PENGUIN BOOKS
TRAPPED

MARTIN VAN BEYNEN was born in Christchurch to Dutch-immigrant parents in 1958. His family moved to West Auckland when he was 11. He studied law at the University of Auckland, graduating in 1981.

After a number of diversions, including working overseas, van Beynen completed a Diploma of Journalism at the University of Canterbury in 1989 and started work with the *Otago Daily Times* in Dunedin.

He joined the *Christchurch Press* in 1991 and after a number of roles was appointed Senior Writer in 2004. His work has attracted several awards, including a 2010 Qantas Media Award ('Story of the Year') for his feature on the trial and acquittal of David Bain, and he was announced Fairfax Media Journalist of the Year 2010–2011.

Van Beynen is married with three children and lives in Diamond Harbour, Banks Peninsula.

TRAPPED

REMARKABLE STORIES OF SURVIVAL FROM THE 2011 CANTERBURY EARTHQUAKE

MARTIN VAN BEYNEN
FOREWORD BY MAYOR BOB PARKER

PENGUIN BOOKS

PENGUIN BOOKS
Published by the Penguin Group
Penguin Group (NZ), 67 Apollo Drive, Rosedale,
Auckland 0632, New Zealand (a division of Pearson New Zealand Ltd)
Penguin Group (USA) Inc., 375 Hudson Street,
New York, New York 10014, USA
Penguin Group (Canada), 90 Eglinton Avenue East, Suite 700, Toronto,
Ontario, M4P 2Y3, Canada (a division of Pearson Penguin Canada Inc.)
Penguin Books Ltd, 80 Strand, London, WC2R 0RL, England
Penguin Ireland, 25 St Stephen's Green,
Dublin 2, Ireland (a division of Penguin Books Ltd)
Penguin Group (Australia), 250 Camberwell Road, Camberwell,
Victoria 3124, Australia (a division of Pearson Australia Group Pty Ltd)
Penguin Books India Pvt Ltd, 11, Community Centre,
Panchsheel Park, New Delhi – 110 017, India
Penguin Books (South Africa) (Pty) Ltd, 24 Sturdee Avenue,
Rosebank, Johannesburg 2196, South Africa

Penguin Books Ltd, Registered Offices: 80 Strand, London, WC2R 0RL, England

First published by Penguin Group (NZ), 2012
1 3 5 7 9 10 8 6 4 2

Copyright © Martin van Beynen, 2012

The right of Martin van Beynen to be identified as the author of this work in terms of
section 96 of the Copyright Act 1994 is hereby asserted.

Photographs © Martin van Beynen unless otherwise stated
Designed and typeset by Anna Egan-Reid, © Penguin Group (NZ)
Map by Geographx Ltd
Printed in Australia by McPherson's Printing Group

All rights reserved. Without limiting the rights under copyright reserved above,
no part of this publication may be reproduced, stored in or introduced into a retrieval
system, or transmitted, in any form or by any means (electronic, mechanical,
photocopying, recording or otherwise), without the prior written permission of
both the copyright owner and the above publisher of this book.

ISBN 978 0 14356723 3

A catalogue record for this book is available
from the National Library of New Zealand.

www.penguin.co.nz

Dedicated to the memory of those who lost
their lives on 22 February 2011

Dr Maysoon Mahdi Abbas, 61
Lalaine Collado Agatep, 38
Dr Husam Sabar Al-Ani, 55
Jane-Marie Alberts, 44
Mary Louise Anne Bantillo Amantillo, 23
Jayden Brytane Andrews-Howland, 15
Emmabelle Cabahug Anoba, 26
Marina Arai, 19
Linda Isobel Arnold, 57
Matthew Lyle Beaumont, 31
Dr Dominic Joseph Gerard Bell, 45
Valquin Descalsota Bensurto, 23
Heidi Julie Berg, 36
Carey Stuart Bird, 48
Andrew James Llewellyn Bishop, 33
Nina Jane Bishop, 32
Pamela (Pam) Maree Brien, 54
Rhys Frank Brookbanks, 25
Melanie Jane Brown, 54
Henry Ross Bush, 75
Ivy Jane Cabunilas, 33
Yu Cai, 31
Ian Neville Caldwell, 47
Cristiano Carazo-Chandler, 35
Helen Margaret Chambers, 44
Yang Chen, 29
John Kristoffer Villegas Chua, 24
Susan Patricia Chuter, 52
Stephen Cochrane, 43
Rachel Elizabeth Conley, 27
Philip Graeme Reeve Coppeard, 41
Patrick John Coupe, 46
Donald Ashby Cowey, 82
Andrew Christian Ross Craig, 46
John Barry (Barry) Craig, 67
Estelle Marie Cullen, 32
Dr Tamara Cvetanova, 42
Betty Irene Dickson, 82
Joanna Clare Didham, 35
Jennifer Ann Donaldson, 55
Paul Clarence Dunlop, 67
Marielle Falardeau, 60
Dian Mary Falconer, 54
Adam Stephen Fisher, 27
Maureen Valerie Fletcher, 75
Ian Foldesi, 64

Jewel Jose Francisco, 26
Samuel Reese Gibb, 27
Jaime Robert McDowell Gilbert, 22
Joanne May Giles, 60
Baxtor Gowland, 5 months
Elizabeth Jane (Jane) Grant, 51
Natasha Sarah Hadfield, 38
Yuki Hamasaki, 23
Xiling Han, 25
Tamara Lia Harca, 59
Jayden Harris, 8 months
Yuki Hasumoto, 22
Yumiko Hata, 29
Miki Hayasaka, 37
Wen He, 25
Jen Jin (Sandra) Hii, 34
Marion Isabella McKirdy Hilbers, 49
Yuko Hirabayashi, 28
Yoshiko Hirauchi, 61
Christopher Grant Homan, 34
Amanda Jane Hooper, 30
Megumi Horita, 19
Hifumi Hoshiba, 41
Siwen Huo, 28
Haruki Hyakuman, 27
Rika Hyuga, 30
Toshiko Imaoka, 34
Gabi Ingel, 22
Thanydha Intarangkun, 36
Tomoki Ishikuro, 19
Kyle Brandon Jack-Midgley, 27
Man Jin, 26
Kayo Kanamaru, 19
Kyoko Kawahata, 20
Beverley Faye Kennedy, 60
Saori Kikuda, 19
Yasuhiro Kitagawa, 39
Chang Lai, 27
Wai Fong Lau, 87
Hsin Hung Lee, 32
Normand Lee, 25
Jin-Yan Leng, 30
Ofer Levy, 22
De Li, 18
Wanju Li, 44
Xia Li, 42

Phimphorn Liangchuea, 41
Adrienne Isobel Lindsay, 54
Haruthaya Luangsurapeesakul, 32
Shawn Charles Lucas, 40
Scott William Emerson Lucy, 38
Catherine McNicol Lunney, 62
Donna Merrie Manning, 43
Kelly Lynn Maynard, 43
Philip John McDonald, 57
Matthew Stuart McEachen, 25
Owen Thomas McKenna, 40
Teresa McLean, 40
Heather Marilyn Meadows, 66
Ezra Mae Sabayton Medalle, 24
Janet Dawn Meller, 58
Adrienne Meredith, 36
Ofer Binyamin Mizrahi, 22
Kelsey Sinitta Moore, 18
Emi Murakami, 19
Jillian Lesley Murphy, 48
Melissa Ann Neale, 41
Erica Avir Reyes Nora, 20
Blair James O'Connor, 34
John Joseph O'Connor, 40
Noriko Otsubo, 41
Linda Rosemary Parker, 50
Joseph Tehau Pohio, 40
Taneysha Gail Rose Prattley, 5 weeks
Wanpen Preeklang, 45
Jessie Lloyd Redoble, 30
Deborah Ann Roberts, 39
Joseph Stuart (Stuart) Routledge, 74
Lucy Routledge, 74
Saya Sakuda, 19
Yoko Sakurai, 27
Jeff Pelesa Sanft, 32
Gillian Sayers, 43
Susan Lyn Selway, 50
Emma Shaharudin, 35
Dr Allan Alexander Sinclair, 45
Christopher Patrick Smith, 48
Christine Patricia (Trish) Stephenson, 61
Reta Stewart, 81
Beverley May Stick, 71
Earl Nicholas Stick, 78

Neil Glyn Stocker, 58
Michael Stuart Coulter Styant, 41
Rhea Mae Sumalpong, 25
Yoko Suzuki, 31
Te Taki (Wally) Tairakena, 60
Hiroko Tamano, 43
Brian Warrington Taylor, 66
Isaac James Thompson, 21
Desley Ann Thomson, 32
Lesley Jane Thomson, 55
Gregory James Tobin, 25
Shane Robert Tomlin, 42
Elsa Torres de Frood, 53
Asuka Tsuchihashi, 28
Hui Yun Tu, 22
Yurika Uchihira, 19
Amanda Jayne (Mandy) Uriao, 38
Valeri Volnov, 41
Jittra Waithayatadapong, 40
Limin Wang, 32
Tao Wang, 29
Graham Weild, 77
Joan Dorothy Weild, 76
Lisa Patricia Willems, 43
Julie Kathryn Wong, 37
Siriphan Wongbunngam, 27
Murray John Wood, 56
Owen Morris Wright, 40
Stephen Robert Wright, 46
Paul Khye Soon Wu, 60
Sisi Xin, 28
Linlin Xu, 26
Xiujuan Xu, 47
Ayako Yamaguchi, 30
Mina Yamatani, 19
Didem Yaman, 31
Caiying Ye, 27
Saki Yokota, 19
Gil Hwan Yu, 23
Naon Yu, 21
Hui Zhang, 34
Weiyu Zhang, 30
Di-Di Zhang, 23
Yantao Zhong, 31
Xioa-Li Zhou, 26

CONTENTS

    Foreword – Mayor Bob Parker   11

    Introduction – Martin van Beynen   13

1   Yukio Minami, Kento Okuda, Rika Iwakura   18
    Third floor, CTV building

2   Amy Cooney   32
    Iconic Bar, corner Manchester and Gloucester Streets

3   Ann Brower   42
    No. 3 bus, Colombo Street

4   Emma Greenslade (née Howard)   52
    Second floor, PGC building

5   David Horsley   64
    Third floor, CTV building

6   Emma Service, Bonnie Singh, Matt Parkin   74
    Southern Ink tattoo studio, Colombo Street

7   Tim Cronshaw   86
    Third floor, *Press* building

8   Ann Bodkin   96
    Third floor, PGC building

9   Chris Littlewood   106
    Sixth floor, Forsyth Barr building

10	Helen Grice **Clyde St, Fendalton**	114
11	Anne Malcolm **Fifth floor, CTV building**	126
12	Marie Mackey **Bennetts Shoe Repairs, Colombo Street**	136
13	Jim Faithfull **First floor, PGC building**	146
14	Qing Tang **Fifth floor, CTV building**	156
15	Ed Post, Gordon Cullen **Fifth floor, Forsyth Barr building**	164
16	Lyn Reid **Third floor, *Press* building**	174
17	Hiroko Sato **Third floor, CTV building**	182
18	Rochelle Prattley, Glenn Prattley **Ruben Blades salon, Lichfield St**	190
19	Sue Spigel **Christchurch Cathedral**	200
20	Ian Reddington **Third floor, *Press* building**	210
21	Kendyll Mitchell, Jett, Dita **Fifth floor, CTV building**	220
22	Jackie Kinder **Southern Ink tattoo studio, Colombo Street**	228
23	David Curtis, Nick Carson **Port Hills and Christchurch Gondola**	236
	Index	246

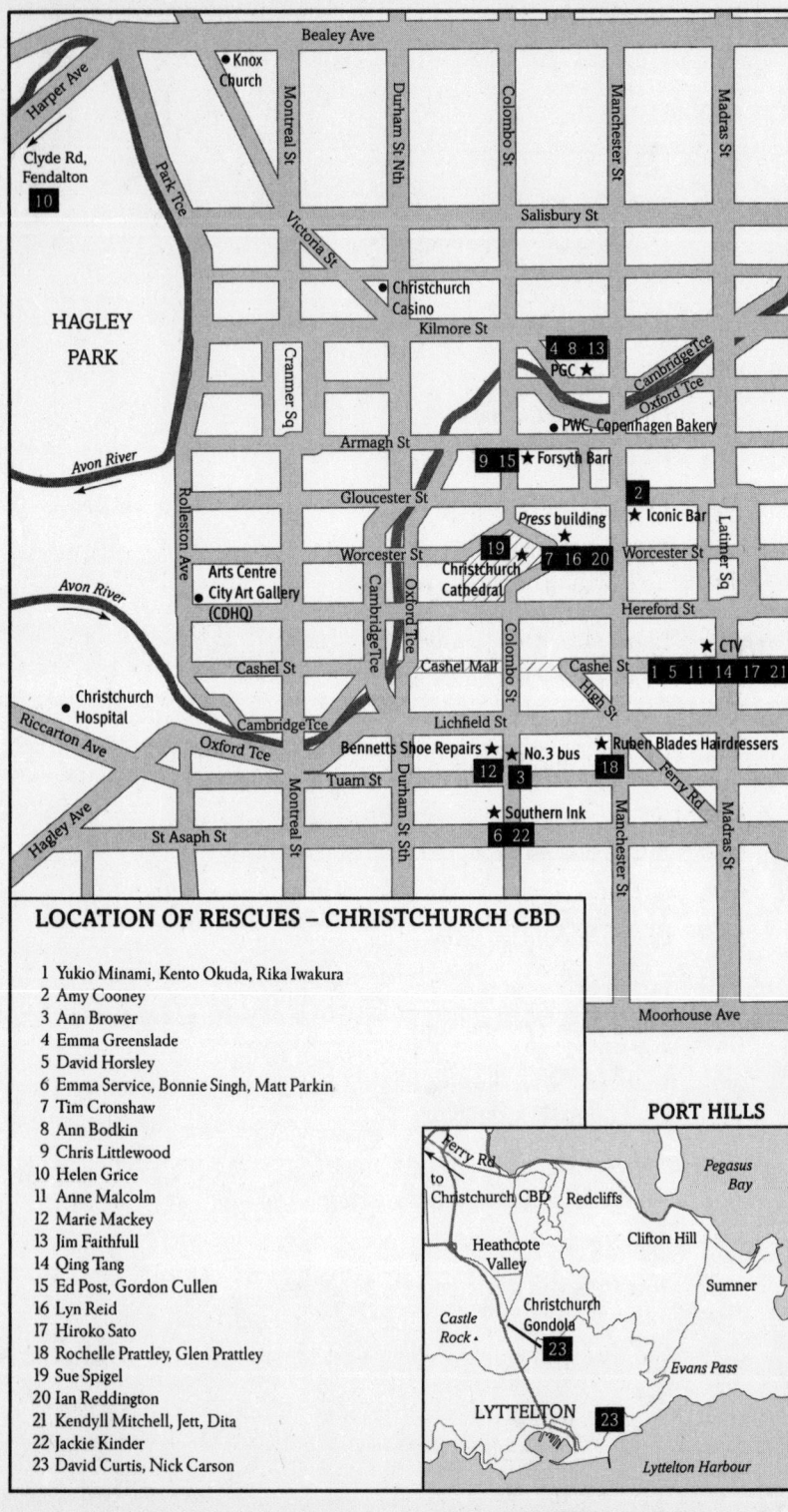

FOREWORD

The morning of 4 September 2010 did not dawn like any other the inhabitants of Canterbury had ever known. In the quiet and still dark of a pre-dawn spring, an earthquake originating near Darfield, on the broad Canterbury Plains, ripped across the checkerboard landscape of farmland and drove straight for the heart of our city. In around 45 seconds of violent shaking the fabric and shape of our lives were changed forever.

Incredibly, in those first seconds of unprecedented seismic violence no-one was killed. A handful of people sustained serious injuries but there were no deaths. We counted our blessings. It was called a miracle. Time went by, and a vision of normality began to return. The earth grew calmer.

Then, six months later, on the afternoon of 22 February, our luck turned for the worse. A massive aftershock blasted from beneath Christchurch: the fault was moving again. That day we lost many souls, crushed in collapsing buildings, others struck by falling rocks. The randomness of this violent event seemed appalling. Most of us recognised the truth of an old saying; 'There but for the grace of God go I.' We all knew the buildings, the hillsides, the streets where lives were lost.

In the days ahead the death toll climbed. It was a process that seemed achingly slow, as rescue teams worked frantically around the clock to find life in the rubble. Many were saved, but many were lost.

Desperate with hope, we were determined to keep searching, sifting the rubble, to leave not one of our people behind. But as each day went past, hope turned to despair as we realised there would be no more miracles of survival in our broken city.

The day came when the number changed no more: 181 souls lost to the quake. The statistic seared into our collective memory like the days, hours and minutes that marked the moments when the quakes had struck.

There is another statistic less well defined and, perhaps strangely, less known. It is the number of those injured by the great quakes and many thousands of aftershocks. Hospital records show only part of the scale of this event, but they indicate that around 250 to 300 people were treated for serious physical trauma in the hours following the February magnitude 6.3 quake. The scale of their suffering seemed somehow lost in the grieving we experienced as a city.

But we need to hear their voices, to understand that for many the impact of the quakes endures. What of those people subject to the most serious physical trauma? Who are they? What are their stories? How are they coping?

In this book, Martin van Beynen presents the stories of some of those for whom life can never return completely to normal. It is their courage, and the courage of those around them, that we must never forget. These are painful but inspiring stories. Our city will rise again, but our recovery will not be complete until we recognise the often unseen toll the earthquakes have taken on those among us who were seriously injured in the great Canterbury earthquakes of 2010/11.

Bob Parker
Mayor, Christchurch City

INTRODUCTION

Everyone who was in Christchurch on 22 February when the 6.3 magnitude earthquake struck with such lethal force is a survivor of sorts. For many the day could have ended very differently. Some had just left for lunch when their building collapsed. Others changed a routine which would have put them in harm's way. Christchurch reporter Emily Cooper was out on a job in Hagley Park when the CTV building in Madras Street, in which she worked, imploded, killing 116 people, 16 of whom were her colleagues and friends.

On 22 February, at 12.51 p.m. when the earthquake hit, I was driving to work at *The Press* newspaper where I was in charge of the late-shift newsroom. The road felt as though it was being stretched in different directions. Further on, rocks the size of settees had crashed on to the road. If I had left home 20 minutes earlier, I might have been unfortunate enough to be under one. In the *Press* building huge chunks of mortar and brick fell on empty chairs and empty desks and although, sadly, one of our staff, Adrienne Lindsay, was killed, the toll could have been much worse. Like me, many people in Christchurch can talk about what might have been had things been only slightly different, but we did not have the sort of dangerously narrow escape most of the people in this book speak of. They are survivors who very clearly cheated death.

Most came very close to being killed by the first jolt or needed to take quick action to improve their chances of survival. Those who weathered the initial carnage but were trapped then had to wait many harrowing hours, knowing they could die at any minute under further collapses triggered by the waves of strong aftershocks following the initial quake.

The stories in this book show graphically how surviving inevitably brings you closer to the dead. In some cases survivors lay trapped next to the dead and dying, and many now find themselves dealing with memories of those, who for no other reason than chance or the arbitrariness of life, did not come home that day. It could so easily have been them. Survivors cannot celebrate life, the fact fate left them alive, without thinking of those who were not so lucky. Many of the survivors in this book lost friends, family and loved ones. They have to cope with the huge gap in their lives and each day the fact that they are still here serves as a reminder of who is not.

There is a belief, and perhaps a well-grounded one, that somehow a near-death experience gives a person an insight or appreciation denied to others. An assumption exists they should have a new lust for life, a newfound determination to make the most of every minute of their precious time. Some whose accounts appear in this book have indeed lived up to this common expectation and look on each day as a gift. Some find their life so altered and transformed they find it hard to embrace it with the enthusiasm expected of them. They might find parts of their altered lives worth living for but they cannot look unsceptically at the glory of each day.

It is unsurprising many of the survivors spent months after the earthquake dealing with anxieties brought on by their experience. Some worry the experience has sown a seed that will wreak havoc later in life. Others look at the world today and wonder 'what next?'. For some, the experience has translated into an unsought and harried alertness to earthquake hazards and a constant need to look for safety and escape. Their stories are a powerful reminder of the unease many Cantabrians live with as a result of three major earthquakes and constant aftershocks in the space of 10 months. They do not trust tall buildings. They do not trust experts. As one survivor explains it, he feels like a huntaway dog sniffing the air constantly for the next disaster.

Some of the survivors have agonised over the question of why they survived when others close to them died. Some feel they have been spared for a reason and must now make the most of life and try to live with more purpose. Others have concluded their survival has no rhyme or reason and as one survivor puts it, 'what is, is'. One believes it is a fruitless question to ask because it has no answer. The question should be, she says, where to go from here.

Survivor guilt is a well-known concept. Many of the survivors felt it – for a short time anyway. Guilt continues to haunt others. A survivor in her sixties feels terrible she survived when so many promising young people with their lives ahead of them were cut down. A father struggles to understand why he is still here while his partner and baby died. Some look back on their actions and ponder the awkward question of whether they could have done more or chosen a better option. It has been hard to avoid the 'what if' questions.

When I started this project I had not thought very much about the ordeal suffered by family and partners of those who so narrowly escaped. As the survivors started to tell their stories, it quickly became evident how waiting to hear about trapped and lost loved ones could be, in its own way, extremely traumatic. Their plight should not be forgotten.

Survival carries all sorts of baggage. A survivor can be someone who has endured through their own bravery and resourcefulness but in the chaos of an earthquake, initial survival is more a matter of being in the right place at the right time. Nonetheless there is still plenty of scope in the immediate aftermath for courage, level-headedness and consideration for others, all features displayed by survivors in this book.

For all the difficulties and burdens survivors must carry and overcome, the survivors who have been generous enough to provide their accounts for this book are, on the whole, glad to be alive. They are testament to the resilience of the human spirit.

I am deeply grateful to the survivors whose stories are recorded in this modest book. They gave of their time, perception and often raw emotion, recounting events which for some of them were still painful to talk about. I wish the injured every strength in their rehabilitation and to those who continue to suffer anxiety and guilt I wish you solace. To all the survivors, I know your stories will inspire others and perhaps bring some comfort to each other.

Many of the survivors were motivated to participate in this book because they wanted to thank their rescuers, medical staff and others who cared for them. So on behalf of the survivors, an enormous thank you to you all.

At Penguin, I thank Jeremy Sherlock for both the opportunity to write my first book and his guidance, Catherine O'Loughlin for her care and attention in all editorial matters, and Anna Egan-Reid for her considered, respectful design. My wife, Paula, cheerfully took up the domestic slack left when I disappeared from the scene, as is necessary when undertaking a project of the scale of a book. She has my deep and heart-felt thanks and appreciation.

Singapore Airlines also gets a resounding vote of thanks for providing a free seat to and from Japan so I could interview survivors in Toyama, where I received the generous and skilled assistance of senior teacher of the Toyama College of Foreign Languages, Susan Urakami. The trust the students had in her made my job much easier.

I thank my editor at *The Press*, Andrew Holden, for allowing the use of several photographs taken by talented *Press* photographers and also for his forbearance in tolerating a reporter whose attention to his paid employment was inevitably somewhat undermined by the distraction of writing a book.

Like the survivors, the city of Christchurch will feel the effects of the 22 February earthquake for a long time. Part of moving forward requires understanding the past. The findings of various inquiries into buildings and structures in which people died will help the survivors as well as the families of the bereaved. The dead and the survivors deserve answers.

I hope this book will also play a small part in recording a moment in a city's history after which life would never be the same.

Martin van Beynen
Christchurch
August 2011

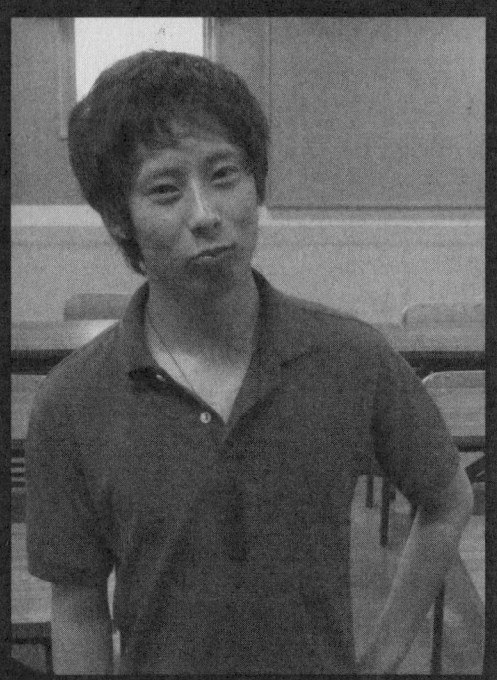
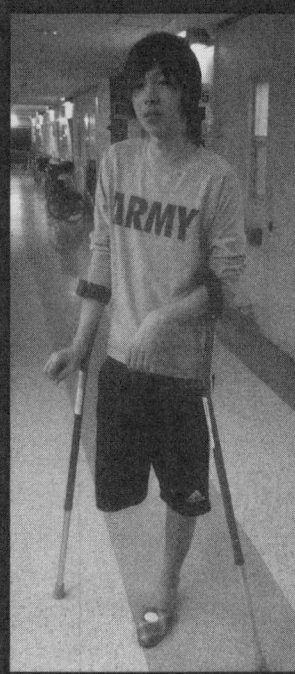
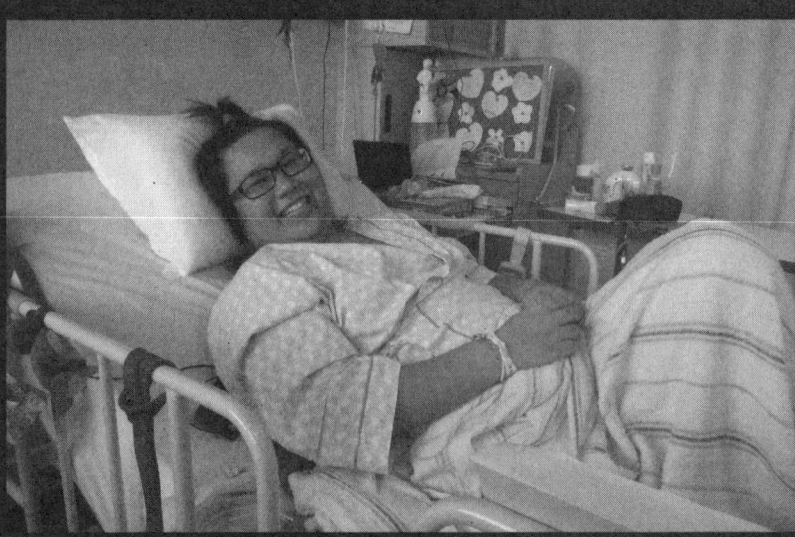

Clockwise from top left: Yukio, Kento, Rika.

1

YUKIO MINAMI
KENTO OKUDA
RIKA IWAKURA

'I only think how I will die.'

MINUTES AGO THEY had been singing a song by the Backstreet Boys led by guitar-playing teacher TeTaki (Wally) Tairakena. Now they were lying in a tangle of bodies, some alive, some dead, some dying, at the bottom of a pile of rubble. The floor of the building they had been on, 2.4 metres in height, had been crushed down to the height of a large book. Acrid smoke wafted through the dark, twisted wreckage.

Kento Okuda, Yukio Minami and Rika Iwakura had been sitting close together at the same cafeteria table laughing and joking while they had their lunch when the earthquake struck. Kento, an avid footballer who captained his high school team, now had one leg trapped beneath a circular concrete pillar. Rika also had a leg pinned by a heavy beam and Yukio lay with a piece of rubble close to his face and two fingers caught. With terrible timing the English language students were in Christchurch for its most devastating earthquake and in its most fragile building. And they were the lucky ones.

The three were part of a 23-strong group from the Toyama College of Foreign Languages (TCFL), who had arrived in Christchurch four days before for a three-week course at King's Education language school, situated on the third floor of the Canterbury Television (CTV) building in Madras Street. The school had been coming to King's Education for three years. Some of the mostly first year students had worked hard to pay for the trip, which had to be privately funded. They were accompanied by two teachers from the school, New Zealander David Horsley (Chapter 5) and Toyama teacher and mother Tomoko Kiyu.

Only 11 of the 23 in the travelling party made it back to Toyama, a city of about 400,000 on the west coast of Japan, about 400 km from Tokyo. Twelve of the group, all students, were killed in the collapse of the CTV building. Another student from Toyama, Kyoko Kawahata, 20, the daughter of TCFL professor Kuniaki Kawahata, was also killed. A university student, she had travelled to Christchurch independently following her father's recommendation of King's Education language school. Of the 116 who died in the CTV building on 22 February, 28 were students from Japan and 64 were students of the King's Education language school. Its principal Brian Taylor and teachers including Te Taki Tairakena and six other staff were also killed.

Yukio was born in Toyama and lives in the nearby countryside with his parents and his sister, who is soon to be married. His parents work for an agricultural co-operative. He enrolled at the Toyama language school, which is the only school of its type in Japan funded by a city government, because he wanted to study business at an American university. Kento also grew up in Toyama and lives with his mother and his older brother Takahiro, 23, who works in a factory. The brothers have always been close. Kento wanted to go to university after leaving school but failed the entrance exam and decided, as Plan B, to study English at the TCFL. When Rika left Toyama Nishi High School she had no firm idea about what she wanted to do. Her mother works in a home improvement shop and her father is a businessman with his own construction company. She has an older brother who plays rugby.

'I didn't have a plan but I would like to visit Canada and America because I went to America once [Oregon and San Francisco] and I had a teacher in high school who was from Canada and she told us lots of things about Canada.'

The students arrived in Christchurch on the Saturday before the earthquake and were taken home by their host families. Rika's family took her to Hanmer Springs and, back in Christchurch, they went for a walk along the beach where a surfing competition was taking place.

Her host mother knew another Japanese student at King's and she got them together for a meal. Another Toyama student on the trip was Yurika Uchihira, 19, Rika's best friend. They had spent three years in the same class at high school and they saw each other every day. 'She was funny. If you spent time with Yurika, you would always be laughing,' Rika says.

Kento's homestay parents took him into town for a ride on the tram and a walk around the city. During the weekend, the Manchester United fan played football with his host family's children at their local school.

Classes at King's started on Monday and the Toyama contingent went on a familiarisation walk through the city as Christchurch turned on one of its best summer days. The following day, Tuesday 22 February, they were allocated classes and all met in the cafeteria before lunch when Wally taught them a Maori stick game and some songs, including the Backstreet Boys number.

'I finished eating and I was sitting and the earthquake started so I started to stand up but it shook so strong I couldn't move any more,' Yukio says. 'I don't remember falling. Something hit me on the head and when I woke up Kento called to me and he said, "Are you OK?" And I said, "I'm OK." It was so dark and I couldn't see anything. I don't know how far away Kento was but when he used his cellphone, I could see the light. I could smell smoke so I thought, *Something is burning*.

'I could hear other people. Some girls were crying and I had pain because my hand was trapped. The fingers were squashed. Just two fingers. I had no space around me. The ceiling was right over my face. I was very scared and uncomfortable. It was not hot but I could smell smoke. I could breathe but I felt terrible. I thought that perhaps I might burn. It was most scary.'

'I had pain because my hand was trapped. The fingers were squashed. Just two fingers. I had no space around me.'

Yukio could hear the voices of the others buried under the rubble asking each other if they were OK. He had a cellphone in his pocket but could not reach it and his movement was very restricted. He could move only his right leg, his left hand and his head a little.

'I kept silent. I said nothing but once I smelt the smoke I asked everyone, "Can you see fire?" I asked that many times. I was trying to sleep. I thought if I slept I wouldn't feel anything terrible. I was just waiting for help. It was just dark with dust and smoke. Also, I could smell oil or something like it. I had no watch, but Kento told me the time. I was lying for I don't know how long before someone came, but it was a very long time. I only think how I will die.'

Kento was sitting next to his teacher Tomoko Kiyu and his friend Yukio at the cafeteria table. 'I was eating a sandwich when the earthquake started. I didn't know what was happening. I held onto the table a bit and then it was like the floor was pulled out from underneath me. Next thing I knew it was all dark and my leg was really painful. Both legs were pinned and it was very painful but I managed to pull one leg out.

'There was a lot of noise at the beginning and a lot of smoke. People were screaming. Ms Kiyu was behind me and my head was on her arm. My leg was really painful but later it didn't hurt so much. I could move my arms maybe sixty centimetres above me but right next to me Ms Kiyu had less space. I couldn't see what was on my leg. I think it may have been a pillar but I couldn't see anything.'

Since his arms were free he was able to reach into his pocket for his cellphone and he called his brother.

'I told him what had happened. That there had been an earthquake and it was pretty serious and could he call somebody to rescue us. He didn't believe me so I let him talk to Ms Kiyu. When I got the phone back I told him my leg was pinned and he told me to just hang on. When the phone rang again it was a New Zealander and I couldn't understand, so I gave the phone to Ms Kiyu.'

Kiyu spoke to rescuers and tried to give them a location. She

Barry Grottis ministers to Anne Malcolm after she was helped from the collapsed CTV building. GEOFF SLOAN, *CHRISTCHURCH STAR*

Kendyll Mitchell is carried out of the wreckage of the CTV building. Daughter Dita in foreground.
GEOFF SLOAN, *CHRISTCHURCH STAR*

Taken minutes after the earthquake. CARYS MONTEATH, *THE PRESS*

Fire still smouldering at the CTV site, late afternoon on 22 February.

also spoke to the school in Toyama and tried to explain what had happened. Then they waited. It was smoky and hot in the part of the rubble in which Kento was entombed. No light relieved the darkness and every minute seemed like an hour. Later water found its way under his body and wet his back. While he waited he talked to the people around him. 'I could hear three or four other students from school and the teacher. They all survived. People around me were shouting but I didn't.'

Rika's host mother had given her a sandwich and instant noodles for lunch, and she was sharing the noodles around when the quake struck. 'It had the same taste as Japan and everybody wanted to eat it. Everyone was having a taste and while that was going on the earthquake started. I might have been standing. I remember it shaking and the next moment I was suddenly lying down. When it started to shake everyone started screaming and I think I saw things falling off the shelves, like the microwave oven.'

She remembers falling and then lying in the dark. 'From there I heard the voices of several people so we could talk to each other a little bit. We were wondering if we were going to be rescued or not. I thought the building had collapsed completely and other buildings around must have collapsed as well. We wondered when they would be able to come if they were helping other people. I couldn't move my legs but I could move the upper part of my body. My legs were painful and both were trapped. The right leg was very painful but I had something on my stomach so I could not see what was on my leg.'

She was lying next to Yurika, could see the bottom of Yukio's foot and could hear teacher Tomoko Kiyu talking to people on the phone. The students would relay the latest news down the line. She could hear people crying out in pain and others calling for help. Her right leg slowly went numb. Rika says she did not think she was going to die but she smelled smoke and worried about the danger it posed. The aftershocks increased the pressure of the weight on her stomach and initially she could hear the voices of some of her friends but then they fell silent. She agonised over why. After a while, she has no idea how long, she saw a light coming from rescue workers and realised she would be saved.

'All the time I was under there I was thinking, *When can I get out?* Sometimes I sang Japanese rock songs, but not out loud.'

It took about six hours before rescuers burrowed their way to where Yukio was lying and it would be another two or so hours before he was able to walk out under his own steam. He could hear them trying to help his fellow student Norika Masutani who was found still in her chair, bent right over in a foetal position under the rubble and panicking. The equipment used to extract Norika put extra pressure on him and he thought he was going to die.

'I told the rescue person, "Please, please, help me first." Norika took such a long time, I got angry. But he said, "Norika first. Then I help you." I said, "OK." Her foot was caught and they couldn't get it out.'

Rescuers believed they would have to amputate Norika's foot which was caught under a steel beam. However after drilling through the floor beneath her foot, they managed to get webbing around the foot and pull it free.

Yukio told the rescuers his name. 'They said, "I'm Louis," and I said, "No, I am Yukio," and they said, "OK, I'll call you Louis from now on." I liked Louis. I was pressured by the pillar so the rescuers used something to lift it. My fingers could come out, and rescuers grabbed my legs and pulled. All the time I was under there I was thinking, *When can I get out?* Sometimes I sang Japanese rock songs, but not out loud. I was thinking those songs in my brain.'

Kento was the last of the group to be reached and he was able to tell rescuers there was nobody alive behind him. Fireman Paul Rodwell shone his torch on the spot where his leg was trapped and saw Kento's leg had been crushed within a 10-mm gap under the pillar. He offered

Kento an injection of painkiller but the student said he was all right. Paul was amazed at his calmness and stoicism.

Kento realised his leg might have to be amputated. 'It was just terrible but I thought it couldn't be helped.'

The fireman gave him water, a torch and oxygen and then withdrew as it had been decided to cut down through the rubble to Kento and then perform the amputation.

'There were a lot of rescuers and they shook my hand and told me to hang in there. It was easy English so I understood. The doctor came and said, "We have to do this." Before the doctor came they tried to pull something off my leg with a rope but it didn't work. The doctor said, "We have to cut the leg off." He tried to put some kind of tube in my leg but he couldn't find a vein, so then they had some kind of a drill. Then I just fell asleep.'

Rika, who was brought out into the night air about 7 p.m., knew Yurika had been removed from the rubble before her but did not know she had died. 'I couldn't see what they were doing but heard the noise of cutting. I can't remember what they were doing. When the weight came off my stomach and legs I had no change in feeling. You would think it would be different but it still felt numb. I was pulled out by my legs first and it was painful but I was really happy I was saved. My leg then started getting much more painful.'

By the time Yukio got out of the building it was night-time and raining and, later, his home-stay mother came to pick him up from Christchurch Hospital.

'I felt sorry but I also felt lucky. When we got home there was no water. I changed my clothes first and watched the news. I drank water and I slept. I had a dream about my friends who came to New Zealand with me. I woke up next morning at 11 a.m. and I watched the news, ate lunch and watched the news again.'

He had called his mother in Toyama from the hospital, using his still intact cellphone. Although he knew some of his friends had died he was delighted to learn that Kento had survived and went to see him and Norika in hospital. 'We talked about the toilet because we had no water at the house and the news was saying, "Don't flush the toilet."'

When Kento awoke in a haze in Christchurch Hospital, the first thing he did was look at his leg. *I don't have a leg*, was his immediate thought. He remained in Christchurch Hospital for six days and, using a wheelchair, was able to visit other injured students. 'The doctors and nurses were very good. Everybody was really kind.'

He flew back to Japan on Air New Zealand, business class, and then spent a week in Tokyo Hospital. His mother joined him in Tokyo and he was relieved to be back. When he returned to Toyama he had to sneak out of the hospital in the middle of the night to avoid Japanese media. His doctor gave him a hat to hide his face.

On the day after the earthquake Rika was flown to Wellington Hospital by helicopter. She went straight to intensive care and she noticed paper cranes, pictures of Hello Kitty and Totoro, a famous Japanese character, above her bed. She doesn't remember much else, as she was heavily medicated.

By Friday, by which time her mother had flown from Toyama to be at her bedside, Rika's kidneys had shut down and she was put on dialysis. On the tenth day of her stay in Wellington Hospital, she went into theatre for some exploratory surgery. During the operation it was decided her leg could not be saved and it was amputated at the hip.

'I still felt it even after they amputated. I didn't know they were going to amputate and only found out when my mother told me. I kind of thought they would do that at some stage but I still thought everything would be OK. I was happy just to have survived. It was a miracle I had survived. I was told that, so it was OK. It could not be helped.'

At first, during her stay in hospital, she did not think too much about her ordeal. Then it began to dawn on her that many of her friends had died. She had no way of contacting her surviving friends and began to feel distressed, lonely and bored. She could not understand the language on the television programmes, so watched cartoons because the English was simple. But then she received a cellphone and her friends wrote her letters, and this helped her feel better. An official from the Japanese Embassy brought her some Japanese comedies on DVD and she enjoyed those. She returned to Japan in early April and shortly after began another series of operations. By June she had notched up nine of them.

'I feel a bit stronger,' she says in early June at Chua Hospital, a large institution on the outskirts of Toyama. 'My muscles are coming back. In the beginning I couldn't move my arms and legs. I am practising standing up on one leg. I use a wheelchair to go most places although I don't go far. I'm not really thinking about the future. My goal is to get back to school. I don't know what I want to do eventually but I want to keep learning English.'

Yukio returned to Japan a week after the earthquake, flying business class courtesy of Air New Zealand. Some of the parents of his friends still thought their children could be alive so he did not give any media interviews. He stayed at home and watched television, mainly comedies. 'My home was too peaceful as I got back to normal life. Too quiet. I knew that in New Zealand life was not normal and I felt bad for my friends who were alive.'

He returned to classes at the language school about a month later. The other students don't treat him any differently. 'A lot of my friends are not there. I just think this classroom is spacious. It was good to be back because I can talk with friends and I don't have to think about bad things. I feel better. I feel OK now, but not strong.'

Yukio is keen to come back to Christchurch but jokes that he will come back with a helmet. 'Christchurch was a good place and my host family was very kind. I need to come back to say thank you to the rescuers and my foster family. I'm not angry. I want to know why the building collapsed but I don't feel angry for the building. Sometimes I can't sleep and think about friends but not so many times.'

He will finish the two-year course in 2012 and then hopes to study in the United States.

In Koshi Rehabilitation Hospital in Toyama, Kento sleeps after an exhausting day of massage, exercise and practising with his new leg. His mother, Hamako, works as a cook in a nearby hospital and she comes to visit each night to bring him clean laundry and treats. Sometimes Kento has phantom pains in the nonexistent part of his right leg and when he complains about the pain, Hamako massages the leg down to his stump. She jokes, 'I tell him now my hand is sore. I ask him, "Can you rub my hand?"'

Her son has his low periods but picks up again quickly, she says. The fact friends who survived were able to visit him in Christchurch Hospital helped him a lot. 'But he felt bad coming back to Japan and leaving his friends behind.'

'I've got kind of used to it,' Kento says of his new leg. 'The first time I couldn't stand up. Now I can walk but it looks kind of funny. Maybe it will get better.'

He says he is not thinking too deeply about his future but thinks he will probably go back to school and try to get into a university. He was interested in psychology before his accident and the counselling he received has made him think about a career as a counsellor. His main ambition at the moment is to get a new driving licence so he can take his little Daihatsu for a spin.

Losing his leg, he says, has changed his attitude towards disabled people. He used to feel sorry for them and now he understands they are trying hard and getting on with life. He admits to having some bad moments after the earthquake but says he remains cheerful and upbeat. He still regards his Christchurch trip as unfinished business.

He has no hard feelings about Christchurch and wants to see the things he didn't get a chance to see. Nor does he want retribution against those responsible for the collapse of the building.

'I'm keen to know why it collapsed but not that keen. It's not that I don't think about it. It's just that it is not that important to me. Maybe the families of the deceased feel that way but I don't.'

Rika would also like to revisit Christchurch and still wants to go to Queenstown. She is not afraid. 'Being in high-rise buildings like the hospital does not worry me. If there was an earthquake and shaking, then I would be afraid. I don't think about [the ordeal] often. I am a happy person and always had friends around. Always talking. I don't feel I have changed although I think my friends who survived have changed. Yurika's death has left a big gap in my life. When I go back to school I will feel the reality of that much more.'

She finds the rehabilitation very tiring and sleeps a lot. She has to strengthen her arms because she has to use crutches and her new leg has yet to be made. Soon she has new visitors and goodbyes must be said. The visitors are family of her fellow King's student, the young woman with whom she had dinner at her host mother's house in Christchurch an age ago. The girl did not come home.

FOOTNOTE: Kento, Yukio and Rika were interviewed with the kind assistance of translator Susan Urakami, a senior teacher at TCFL.

2

AMY COONEY

'I must have been knocked out for two or three minutes. When I came to, I couldn't figure out why I couldn't move.'

A TOUCH UNDER the rubble. A hand. It belonged to Amy Cooney's brother Jaime Gilbert. *Sweet*, she thought. *I've got my brother.* That feeling would fade quickly. Concussed, injured and buried in a pile of broken stone and steel that twisted her head and body, Amy called for help. Her thoughts were all for Jaime. She couldn't feel any movement coming from him.

Three months later, Amy is living with her partner and three children in a Woolston street still bearing the scars of February's earthquake. On a May afternoon, she is bottle-feeding a baby she is caring for until his grandmother in Australia can come to collect him. Later her twelve-year-old son Jesse comes home from school. He is wearing sneakers several sizes too big for him and Amy explains he chose his Uncle Jaime's shoes when some of his belongings were passed down to family members.

And it seems they are big shoes to fill in another sense too as Amy describes the brother who was killed. 'Everybody loved to be around him. He was just one of those lights. You couldn't wait for him to arrive at a family gathering. Having him around made you feel good.'

Jaime Gilbert was only 22, the partner of Natalie O'Brien and father of India, then about six months, and Levi, 2, when he was struck by the crumbling façade of the Iconic Bar, on the corner of Manchester and Gloucester Streets in central Christchurch, in the earthquake of 22 February.

Amy had picked him up that morning from a friend's place. It was their first official day together at the bar, which Amy was managing. She has worked in the hospitality industry since school and has managed pubs, cafés, night clubs and bars. She and Jamie often worked together because Amy would get Jaime jobs while he was at school and later when he studied at the National Academy of Singing and Dramatic Art at the Christchurch Polytechnic.

Their friend Leanna Christie had taken over the Iconic Bar only three weeks before and had lured Amy out of partial retirement to run it. 'We had so many plans. We were looking forward to the World Cup and Jaime was going to be the day manager. We were excited and so looking forward to working together again after about two years, making some money for our friend and having a good time doing it.'

Her brother liked to cram so much into 24 hours it was surprising he could stay awake, she says. At the time of his death he worked fulltime, came home to put the kids to bed, was rehearsing the play *Hamlet* directed by his father Robert Gilbert, and in which he played Laertes, and was making a television programme with his mother. 'He was a different kettle of fish, this boy. You can imagine how close he was to us all and what a big loss he really is.'

When the earthquake struck at 12.51 p.m., Jaime was doing a stocktake behind the bar and Amy, who had been counting money in the safe room, had come over to chat and was standing at the counter like a patron. 'I heard it first. I felt like I could hear it coming down the hill, down Manchester Street. I have really sensitive hearing and I felt the vibrations. It was like a 747 right on the street. I looked at my bro and I thought we had to get out. Things were falling down around us and I assumed getting out of the building was safer than staying in. He was one or two steps behind me.'

She was out the door, which was buckling and shifting, just ahead of Jaime. Three other people were in the building but all managed to get out without injury. 'I knew things were shifting. We were all on the footpath. There were two cars parked directly outside the door and I was trying to get to the intersection because it had to be safer. My brother was right there and he yelled out to me, "Come here. Get over here." He reached over to put his arm around me. He must have seen the top of the building start to fall off and down to the footpath.

He went to reach out and I heard him yell and I tried to grab him and that is when the entire front face of the building came down.'

The façade of plaster, limestone and steel buried them both. Amy was knocked unconscious but a car parked next to her took some of the force of the falling debris and probably saved her life. 'I must have been knocked out for two or three minutes. When I came to, I couldn't figure out why I couldn't move. I couldn't figure out where I was or what had happened. I hadn't even remembered the earthquake. I was like, *Hey, what the hell has happened?*'

Amy was pinned under the dirt and rubble with her backside and hip on the edge of the footpath. Her face was covered in dust and blood and she struggled to marshal her thoughts.

> **Pumped up with adrenalin, he picked up large limestone blocks and threw them aside like he was Superman.**

'Then I felt my brother's hand. I thought, *I'd better get someone to get me out*. It was all dark and my neck was twisted and I couldn't see anything. I was calling out but it was very hard to focus. I was getting no reply and my heart was racing and I was getting more panicky. Then I heard Sam [Siave], who was also working in the bar, saying, "I can hear you, Amy. I'm coming for you."'

At this time Ashei Sopoaga, a Samoan father of four from Little River on the south side of Banks Peninsula, arrived to help. Pumped up with adrenalin, he picked up large limestone blocks and threw them aside like he was Superman. His actions were captured on film and, with the footage being shown around the world, he became something of an overnight hero.

Amy was still desperately calling for Jaime. 'I felt a last movement. I was pretty sure he was critically injured. I thought he had passed away. I kind of felt it. Sam was pulling stuff off me. I was guiding him where and what to pull off because it hurt too much when he took some bits off. At the same time I was saying, "Make sure you get my bro." Finally he got whatever was on my head, neck and shoulders off so I could lift my head up. I still had my legs pinned. I saw my brother's hand. I was still holding it so it was good to see his hand was there and then they got my legs free and moved to my brother.'

An aftershock brought more debris down on the footpath and rescuers jumped clear. Two women, also from Little River, tried to move her away but Amy resisted strongly. 'I was screaming for my brother and blood was coming down my face. They moved me to the middle of Manchester Street and they wanted me to sit on their jacket and I was getting furious. "Don't take me away," I said.'

Reassured by Sam, Amy stood on the road watching Ashei throw the blocks around. 'The next thing, I saw Sam scooping him up. He was lying face down and Sam got his hands under his body and carried him like a child and brought him over to me.'

The priority was to get them both to hospital as soon as possible. As though sent by fate, two electricians arrived in a van and quickly made room in the back for both Jaime and Amy.

Police officer Spencer Kingi, who had helped extricate Jaime, had already taken his pulse and Amy took it again, but she knew he had gone. 'His face was smashed in. He had lots of blood on his lips and his face was covered in dried blood and I kept cleaning his face. I was pretty much lying beside him, curled up beside his body and there was no life in him.'

The trip to the hospital in the van was, says Amy, like a movie. One of the men ran in front clearing rubble and people out of the way while the other drove all over the road and footpath honking his horn as he went. Outside the police station in Hereford Street, two officers jumped in the van and tried to resuscitate Jaime without success.

'The driver was frantically trying to get to the hospital. The sliding door was open and I was holding on to a bar. I had all these injuries and didn't know what was wrong with me. I was trying to hold it together. I can remember the look on people's faces like, *Wow, what the hell had happened?* I remember looking towards to the hills through the rubble and thinking, *How on earth are we going to deal with this?'*

Amy makes light of her injuries but she had cuts to her head, a fractured cheekbone, torn muscles, chipped ankles and was covered in bruises, which on later examination showed the imprints of bricks and beams.

The hospital was in chaos when they arrived but a police officer scooped up Jaime's body and took him inside and Amy hobbled after him. 'I wasn't conscious of my body. I was only worried about my brother's body and making sure he was safe. I didn't feel my physical injuries until Jaime's body was taken away from me.'

All the available beds were taken so Jaime was laid on the floor of an ambulance where doctors began attempts to resuscitate him after pulling the curtains shut. 'I said, "Don't shut me out. I need to know what is going on. I need to be a part of this."'

Finally a nurse approached to say the doctors could not do any more for Jaime and he had passed away. 'I looked at her, trying to take it all in, and I said, "It's all right. He's safe now." They had found a bed for him and I was on the bed with him and just kept cleaning up his face and talking to him and I was crying and said goodbye to him for all my family and my friends. I thought of all the people who wanted to say goodbye to him and said goodbye on behalf of them. I was praying. I'm not religious. I'm spiritual. I grew up with parents who were Bahai and it does give me lots of grounding and general spiritual awareness. I do believe in an afterlife.'

Jaime, she says, was deeply interested in a number of religions and also his Maori background. His grandfather was connected with the Wairewa marae in Little River, where Jaime is buried. The two women who helped Amy outside the bar now tend his gravesite.

Although Amy has coped remarkably with the death of her brother, the impact of her shocking experience continues to reverberate. She says she is very anxious and jumps at any little noise or rumble. Her heart races and takes a long time to get back to normal.

'I'm not a nervous person. I'm usually confident and self-assured. The day before Jaime's funeral I went to Hornby Mall to buy some clothes for the kids and I had a panic attack from being in a large building with people around me. I was out of breath and overheating. That's never happened to me. I'm so not that sort of person and it's such a shock.'

She has coped with the aftermath by talking about the accident as often as possible. 'I assume there is greater force that knows better than I do and for my own survival and my children I have to accept that is so, and trust I will meet my brother again on a spiritual plane. He will be able to guide me because he will be light years ahead of me when I'm going to die.

'I still feel his love. Just because he is not here, his love does not stop. So knowing his love is here is just tremendous. Sometimes in my head, it's like he is sitting beside me. Anything that makes me feel closer to him makes me feel good. If things are hard, like a bad moment with the kids, I think in my head as if he is there and it gives me a moment of relief. I owe it to my brother to live the dreams that we dreamt. It's compulsory.'

Amy did not forget all those who helped on the day and has made a point of going back and thanking everyone who played some part in trying to help her and Jaime. 'That's what strikes you when you are in this situation. Everybody helps you. It's just amazing what people do. It taught me to be more conscious of my effect on other people and be more helpful and sympathetic and understanding. To live each day gratefully.'

'That's what strikes you when you are in this situation. Everybody helps you. It's just amazing what people do.'

She wants to live a more positive and helpful life. 'I'm gutted that I don't have my bro here to hang out with and give a hug to and pour my heart out to, but I'm also thankful to be alive and I have to honour him and honour me and my children and my family to ensure the way I live my life from now on is with purpose and not just nine to five. I want to make a difference in people's lives, to show that I'm grateful that I'm alive in a protective, motherly, nurturing kind of way.'

While she is philosophical about what happened to her brother, she is angry about one thing. 'I get wild when I think he should be here with his children because he was an amazing, awesome father.'

Amy has decided to move to Brisbane with her family, partly to be closer to her remaining brother, Steve. 'I don't feel that I need to be loyal to Christchurch any more. I think Christchurch has taken enough out of me for now. I feel I continually have to be on my toes and one step ahead of Mother Nature. I feel I have to run and hide to protect my children. I'm always on edge, even with the washing, which I feel I have to get on to in case we run out of water.'

Amy looks at the time. She needs to think about tea for the children and she is going out. Tonight is the opening night of *Hamlet*, which is being performed at the Aurora Centre at Burnside High, Jaime's old school. Jaime's father and Amy's stepfather, Robert Gilbert, who lived with the family until she was 16, is both directing the play and stepping into the role of Laertes, the part his son was to play.

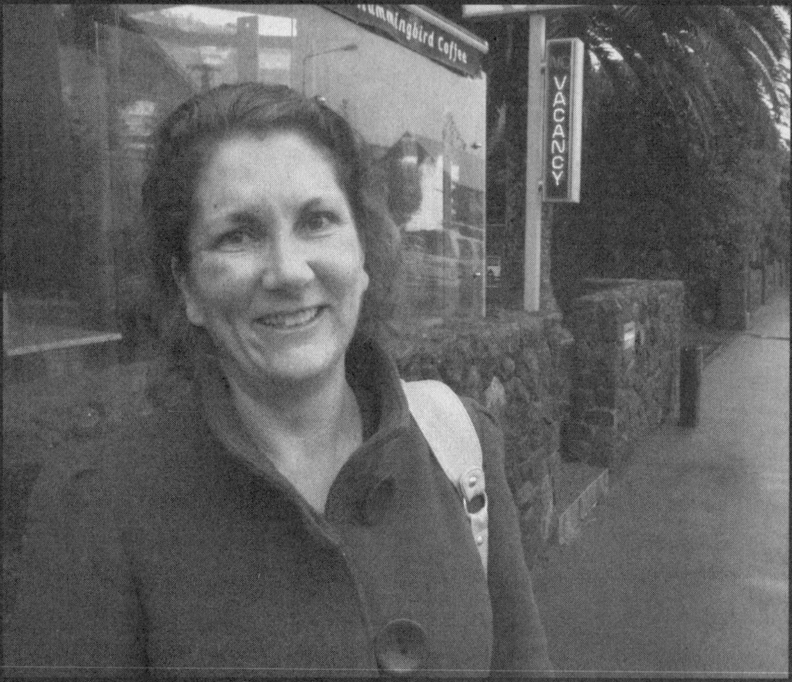
VACANCY

3

ANN BROWER

'I remember more and more pressure coming on and thinking, *I don't know how much more I can take.*'

SOMETIMES THE PAIN was too much and she passed out. Only seconds before, she had been sitting happily in the No 3. bus from Sumner, but then the quake had struck and now the roof of the bus was squashed by tonnes of rubble from the adjacent building. It was pressing down on her hips, having already broken her leg and several bones in her hand as it had buckled. She was too jammed in and restricted to look around, and although she couldn't know it at the time perhaps that was just as well because eight other people on her bus had lost their lives, probably instantly. Ann Brower was the only survivor in the No. 3 bus.

The drive to Ann Brower's suburb of Sumner, which sits under the Port Hills by the coast, is a graphic reminder of February's earthquake. The hill suburbs are littered with broken homes and tile roofs scattered like a jigsaw puzzle. The road is bumpy, the bridge under repair and the lethal cascades of rocks from the brittle cliffs have yet to be cleared away. A massive trench has been dug to put in a new sewer, some hill streets have been evacuated and the Redcliffs supermarket, a landmark on the No. 3 bus route, has been demolished.

Brower, 40, is also still a little broken. Her left leg, which was badly gashed and broken in the earthquake, is healing although a skin graft is causing problems. The broken bones in her left hand are also mending and she hopes to play her violin again soon, but her pelvis, which was fractured in a number of places, still hurts.

Ann went tramping over the weekend before the earthquake and drove back on Monday thinking she should have stayed another day. On Tuesday she got on the bus in Sumner for a trip to Canterbury University to meet up with a colleague with whom she was collaborating on a paper about land sale prices. She lectures in environmental and social policy at Lincoln University and most of her recent research has been about New Zealand's controversial high country tenure review, on which she has often spoken in the media.

A native of North Carolina, she came to New Zealand on a Fulbright grant in 2005 after finishing her doctorate at Berkeley University in California.

'I always took the bus to Canterbury [University] because you can't park there and I can read a magazine while I travel. I think I missed the bus I wanted to be on. I was reading the *Economist* and the bus was between Tuam and Lichfield Streets. I wasn't paying attention to who was on the bus and no-one was sitting next to me. I wanted to be on the sunny side of the bus. It was such a beautiful day and I thought I will just sit in the sun and read my magazine. The bus stopped and I looked up and it started shaking back and forth really violently and I thought, *Yep another aftershock, not liking that in town.* I had a perverse thought about at least getting to see what it was like in town. Then I saw bricks falling. The wheels of the bus were coming off the ground.'

The bus was heading north towards the bus exchange in Lichfield Street and the bricks came from façades to the left of Ann, who was on the side of the bus closest to the centre of the road.

'I braced myself against the seat in front on me. I think at that point I fainted because my leg and pelvis would have broken then. The roof was on my hips. All the weight was on them. I don't remember the impact but I remember more and more pressure coming on and thinking, *I don't know how much more I can take.* I was screaming, "No. No. No." That was the only point I thought I might not make it out of there. I think I passed out again.'

'Rob talked about fishing and he told me later his plan was to get me to focus solely on him because of what was around us.'

When she did come to she found the window next to her intact and began knocking on it to let people know she was alive in her little pocket in the bus. 'I am a trained lifesaver. I know to raise my hand.'

The predicament of the people on the bus attracted an instant rescue crew and immediately work began on removing the debris from the roof of the bus. 'Every time they took a huge chunk off the roof I screamed in pain. They sent an emissary down from the roof to say hello to me through the window. The first sign of life I remember was a fluoro vest. He came down every couple of minutes and I was saying, "I'm fine. Get the others." During the screaming time I was wriggling my toes and I thought, *Please let this not be spinal*. I was able to wriggle them and that reassured me it probably wasn't spinal and maybe my leg was not broken.'

Ann could not see her injuries but her hand was bleeding from a cut tendon and the broken bone in her leg had come through the skin. She doesn't remember being in excruciating pain and could not see her fellow passengers. One rescuer was to describe the carnage inside as a 'butcher's shop'.

'The difference between me and the other people on the bus was nothing much landed on my head. Just knowing people were coming was quite huge. Pretty soon after [about 10 minutes after the earthquake] Rob [Green] somehow crawled in. The idea of him crawling into a crushed bus to comfort someone is extraordinary.

'It took about 30 to 40 minutes to get the rubble off the bus. There was so much. The guys could walk from the footpath to the roof of the bus. Rob talked about fishing and he told me later his plan was to get me to focus solely on him because of what was around us. We just had a conversation although I can't remember many of his answers. We talked about the basic things and I remember talking about where we lived. Just anything at that point was comforting.'

After part of the roof was ripped off, one of the rescuers plucked Ann from her seat and she was passed overhead to the street. 'Apparently they asked me to wriggle my fingers and toes. No ambulance staff were there. They splinted my leg and I passed out again.'

Ann was reluctant to let Rob leave but he went to get her bag from the bus and was not able to see her again until three days later. Because the bag contained Ann's cellphone, he had to answer worried calls from her friends.

On the trip to the hospital in a four-wheel-drive vehicle her companions introduced themselves and Ann demanded one of them tell a funny story. 'It was about a funny place in England with a funny name. I didn't quite get it but I laughed because I thought I should laugh now.'

Her hospital record shows she arrived at the hospital about 1.50 p.m. when 'morphine was delivered'. Her early arrival meant she at least got a hospital bed.

'I remember being bowled over by how calm the staff was. They were just amazing. The lights were flickering on and off. One of the guys stayed with me for about two hours and a medical student stayed with me after that. We made bets on what was wrong with me. I was really lucky to have her with me. They splinted my leg and I remember that being exquisitely painful.'

After ringing her parents in the United States, she went into theatre as a high priority patient due to the compound fracture to her leg and a broken bone in her hand.

The recuperation did not go entirely smoothly. 'The first week in hospital was rough because they were trying to get me up on crutches and I was just screaming in pain. I just couldn't put any weight on either foot. They sent the psych team in, thinking I may be traumatised but I was just a little pissed off. I also have a high tolerance for pain. I wanted like anything to stand up but I can't describe the pain. Eventually I got another doctor and they discovered I had a number of breaks in my pelvis and needed bed rest for six weeks.'

She spent two weeks in Christchurch Hospital and after two operations was moved to Burwood Hospital for five weeks' recuperation and rehabilitation. Prior to the earthquake she had never spent a night in hospital. 'Burwood was like heaven. It's like a hotel with nurses. I had been in a room with six other people and it was always hot. The first week [in Christchurch Hospital] was mainly earthquake people. Then we started to get more non-earthquake injuries and they seemed to complain more and ask for things more.'

In early June, Ann is so busy with physiotherapy she has no time for work. She is planning a party for the men who took part in her rescue from the bus. She hasn't been bothered by many nightmares and believes she exorcised most of her trauma in the first week, although she recalls that one aftershock did give her a terrifying flashback.

'I can't describe the pain. Eventually I got another doctor and they discovered I had a number of breaks in my pelvis and needed bed rest for six weeks.'

'I'm too busy with physio to think too much about it. I knew almost straight away they were coming for me. I grew up religious. I did think about that on the bus. *Please let this not be spinal* is a prayer whether you say Jesus Christ or Buddha. Before I went into surgery, I asked the medical student to say the Lord's Prayer with me. The trouble with being too philosophical about this sort of experience is you can easily go down the road that you were spared for a reason. The flip side is those people were killed for a reason and I just can't abide with that. Or someone was watching over me. But the flip side of that is someone was not watching over the people who were killed. I believe in a God but not an interfering one.'

She has no problem with going on buses and would sooner do that than go into Colombo Street. She recently met the Dalai Lama, who visited Christchurch to talk to survivors and families of the dead. Ann found it useful.

'As the Dalai Lama says, it's easy to dwell on the "what ifs" and how close you were to death and the others who did not survive. But the point is you did survive and you have lots to look forward to. I have definitely had moments of sadness for the others on the bus.

I don't think I am that philosophical about it. I felt guilty that first week, especially when I got a phone call from the wife of one of those killed. But I can't tell you it's given me a new lease on life.'

Ann says the most moving thing about the day she met the Dalai Lama was meeting the other survivors. 'They were all just courage personified. There are plenty still in hospital. People have forgotten people got injured. They talk about the buildings but there are plenty of us.'

> 'People have forgotten people got injured. They talk about the buildings but there are plenty of us.'

Worried the Royal Commission into collapses of buildings like the CTV and PGC building will not scrutinise the façade collapses that killed her fellow passengers and injured her, she wants its scope widened.

'Everyone knew unreinforced brick façades collapse in quakes. New Zealand prides itself on its strong building codes, but the fate of my bus shows the codes are the regulatory equivalent of Swiss cheese. The No. 3 bus tragedy was man-made. We know why they died. Please, someone have the courage to tell us why.'

FOOTNOTE: The Royal Commission of Inquiry into the Canterbury earthquakes did eventually commission a report on unreinforced masonry (URM) buildings in Christchurch. The report recommended all the country's 3867 URM buildings should be strengthened to at least 67 per cent of the latest design requirements, and estimated the national cost at about two billion dollars. The report highlighted poor connectivity between walls at their corners and between façades and their supporting timber diaphragms as causing the sort of collapse which claimed the lives of the people in Ann's bus. It also pinpointed the low quality of some construction materials, including low-strength lime mortar.

Emma and Chris Greenslade at their wedding reception three days after the earthquake. ANDY CURRIE

4

EMMA GREENSLADE (NÉE HOWARD)

'Why couldn't I have just died straight away? It would be so much easier to die straight away than to be sitting there for so many hours and then get crushed.'

IN A CITY REELING from a deadly earthquake and starved of good news, the wedding of Chris Greenslade and Emma Howard shone out as a beacon of hope and normality. Only a few days earlier Emma had been trapped for eight hours in the collapsed Pyne Gould Corporation building in Cambridge Terrace, where 18 people were killed. With no idea whether she had survived, Chris had had to endure an agonising wait outside the building.

It was not surprising then that their wedding, on the Friday after the Christchurch earthquake of Tuesday 22 February, attracted nearly as much attention as the slightly more famous wedding of Prince William and Kate Middleton soon after. Although only a few camera operators were allowed into Burnside's Christ the King Catholic Church, where Emma's grandparents attend mass four times a week, a bank of cameras was waiting for the couple as they left the church. Chris counted 26 media photographers and video cameramen, in addition to various reporters from a myriad of media organisations. 'It was a peek at what the lifestyle of the rich and famous must be like,' says Chris.

Emma did not always enjoy the attention, especially in the morning before the wedding service when she wanted to have time with her friends and do her hair and make-up in peace. Instead she conducted a series of media interviews, including one with a freelance magazine journalist who believed she had found the firefighter who rescued Emma. It turned out to be the wrong rescuer but that did not stop the story going in the magazine.

'I didn't get to relax until I was in the car on the way to the church with Dad. It never crossed my mind that there would be a media frenzy. The most intimidating thing for me was as we were about to leave there was this camera on the [car] window at my face.'

Emma, who is training to be an accounting technician with accounting firm Leech and Partners, had not wanted to go to work in the firm's second-floor office on the day of the earthquake. Although she felt the building was still safe after Christchurch's September earthquake, she had lots of little jobs to do before the wedding and Monday was going to be her last day for the week. However she felt guilty about putting stress on her supervisor, so decided not to ask for the day off. She arranged to go out to lunch with a friend.

Emma was sitting at her desk, somewhere towards the middle of the floor, when the rumbling of the earthquake started. She waited for it to stop.

Chris, an accounting graduate who is doing his professional exams this year (2011), dropped Emma at the PGC building before heading to work. The couple met about three years ago when Chris, straight out of university, joined accounting firm Marriots, where Emma was then working. Emma was going out with her high school sweetheart at the time but after a bust-up that normally would have resolved itself, they did not get back together. 'I already had feelings for Chris,' Emma says.

Within about nine months they had bought a house together and worked towards a wedding. Both grew up in a farm environment. Chris's parents are well known dairy farmers in Lincoln and Emma was raised on a rural block, north of Christchurch. Chris still works every third weekend on the family farm and Emma would dearly love to be a full-time farmer. She has to content herself with two dogs and two cats, helping Chris on his parents' farm and doing a lot of farm accounting.

On 22 February, Chris was busy tidying up loose ends at work in his second-floor Victoria Street office building near the Christchurch Casino. Emma was sitting at her desk, somewhere towards the middle of the floor, when the rumbling of the earthquake started. She had experienced a number of aftershocks in the building and waited for it to stop. Philip McDonald, an Ashburton partner of the firm, who was spending the day in the Christchurch office, was standing in the aisle next to her looking at a file. He was not to make it out of the building alive.

'I sat there staring at Philip standing in the aisle,' says Emma. 'We had blank expressions on our faces. Then everything happened at once. I never saw anything fall. It happened just like that and it was just darkness. I remember grabbing this thing, a pipe, and pulling myself up because I had been thrown off my chair.'

Emma knew she was stuck in a dark hole but could see virtually nothing. A colleague, Annette Burgess, was about five metres away and had a cellphone which lit up the cavern slightly. Emma could hear others but did not know that 12 of her co-workers were still in the office when the earthquake hit. Partner Nick Wall, who was pinned by rubble falling on his back and legs, was not far away and in great pain.

'We straight away worked out who was there and who wasn't. I was talking to Dwayne [Goodall] a lot on the other side of the beam. He was lying down and he was on his back and could not sit up. Next to Dwayne, was Kim [Flintoff] and then Nick [Wall] and Ros [Parker], who was on her first day of work. Glen [White] and Chris [Heffernan] were in their offices. Chris couldn't hear anybody and thought we were all dead.'

Emma had two cameras with her. She took her first picture at 3.30 p.m. and then found she could reach her handbag, which contained her other camera. 'I had a brand new camera which Chris had given me as a wedding present and it was fully charged because I had to learn to use it before the honeymoon.'

When she took photos with the camera, it not only provided her with a lifelong record of her traumatic entrapment but gave her an immediate insight into how and where she was trapped. Annette immediately began to talk to family in Australia and also later sent a text to Emma's parents to let them know she had survived and was uninjured. Chris received a similar text but not before 4 p.m.

In the darkness Emma and her co-workers reeled from the shock. 'I pulled myself up and was sitting in a foetal position. I was sitting on a whole lot of crap, with things digging into my bum but I couldn't move because it was everywhere. Even if I could move I didn't want to in case it dislodged something. We really thought we were going to get squished. We were in darkness for a couple of hours but with the flash from the camera we could see a bit.

'I was just thinking, *Thank God I never moved*. If I had got under my desk, at the very least I would have broken something. Because that corner of the building just smashed it. It's so hard to believe just about everyone was OK, considering. Philip was standing looking at a file before the earthquake but I didn't see anything. I know Kim had to rest her head on his leg.'

An added, hair-tearing-out frustration for Emma was that she could see and hear her cellphone, but couldn't reach it. 'My phone was just in front of me and I could see the dimmest light every time someone rang me and I could hear it vibrate. It must have gone off about 15 to 20 times but I just couldn't get to it. It was sandwiched between goodness knows what and I just couldn't get to it. I was sitting on the ground and had a file on my head for a couple of hours with the aftershocks. It was better than nothing. Nick was being crushed. I could hear him and he was in a lot of pain. I could hear three or four girls underneath me.'

Despite the emergency, nature calls needed to be heeded. 'I peed into my two-minute noodle cup. I was really fortunate to be wearing a dress. Annette peed into her rubbish bin and someone else peed into her shoe. We were too scared. We didn't want to move in case we disturbed something.'

About 6 p.m., to Emma's great relief Steve Rule, a firefighter from the Christchurch Central station, crawled down through the wreckage and managed to make contact with the group. Eventually he got a light into their cave-like cavity. His arrival lifted the group's spirits enormously as they knew the rescue effort was focusing on their group, Emma says.

'For a very long time we had been listening to everybody else get help. It was such a relief to finally be the ones about to get out of there. I didn't think I was going to get out of there until I heard Steve. There was a lot of banging and drilling going on underneath me and I was terrified of that. I thought, *They are going to drill and everything is going to fall on top of me. While trying to get us out or someone else out, everything will fall. Steve cannot get to our floor.* I thought, *Why couldn't I have just died straight away?* It would be so much easier to die straight away than to be sitting there for so many hours and then get crushed.

'We were all talking about it. Kim made a comment about smelling fumes and I said at least you will go peacefully. She didn't think it was funny. I was the most hysterical. I was crying. I went through patches of crying and screaming, "I want to die." Everyone else was trying to be positive.'

A very worried Chris was waiting on the street outside the building. The quake had shaken his own building violently and had been the only aftershock to make him dive for the safety of his desk. After comforting another employee and helping extract some new graduates from shelves of files, he went to pick up Emma.

'I thought she would be upset and wanted to take her home. Her office is only a 15-minute walk away, but in the end I was running. The buildings on the way seemed OK and then I got to Emma's work and there was a flat building. I thought they would all be dead because I knew where they sat. Already a few fire trucks had arrived and they were already doing stuff. About twenty people were trying to help. For about five minutes I was a bit of a wreck and then tried to help and keep moving.'

Chris admits to brief moments of thinking his life would be lived without Emma but he didn't allow himself to think those thoughts for long. 'I just kept moving and helping the firemen and helping people get out. Then the text message came saying, *Emma here and I'm OK and love you very much.* I asked her who else was in there and told her I loved her very much too. That was the point when I thought she was going to get out as the building hadn't moved much in the aftershocks.'

Meanwhile, work on getting through to Emma and her colleagues was progressing well. 'As I was talking to Steve,' Emma says, 'I told him light was coming from behind Annette and then Cory [Stewart] popped his head through the wall.'

In one of those it's-a-small-world coincidences, Cory, another fireman from the central station, plays for the Banks Peninsula rugby team which sometimes competes against the Lincoln team, for which Chris plays flanker. The hole Cory punched through the wall allowed Emma and Annette to escape their cave, although their problems were not over yet.

'To get out to the top of the building I had to walk up the stairs and they were lined with fire brigade people. I had no shoes on. I said, "Glass is fine," and hooned up the stairs. We had to abseil up a part. I got up there and fell into the arms of the Hanmer fire chief and he held me for a long time. I then talked to Steve and he wanted me to confirm where the others were. On top of the building they were all cheering and they were so happy to see me.'

As she came down in a cradle lowered by a crane, she could see Chris running towards her.

'He didn't have tears. He was very calm and quiet. He pulled me out of the crane and he carried me to the ambulance. It was just a huge relief. I had stopped the feelings. I kind of shut down almost because I had been all go for six and a half hours.'

Emma emerged from the building at exactly 7.34 p.m. She had a big bruise on her arm and bruises all over her backside and down the back of one thigh. It was raining and getting cold but she stayed at the site for another two hours to wait for her friend Dwayne to be extracted.

When she and Chris finally came home, sleep was elusive. 'I did not want to go to sleep just in case. I stayed on the couch for about three or four hours and watched the news which had footage of Chris carrying a woman out of the building. It was played a lot.'

The fate of the wedding had already been decided. 'I was on the stretcher and I assumed we wouldn't be getting married and Dad and Chris said, "Yes you are." I wanted to get married and Father John [Adams, the marriage celebrant] was very good about it. We lost our cake, which was coming from a shop the owners could not get into. I didn't care. I thought, *Whatever*. My stepmother made a cake.

'The booklets were not done. Just little things. Wednesday and Thursday were going to be for little stuff. The earthquake moved the focus to the people,' says Emma. 'I stress about the littlest things and before the earthquake I wanted this wedding to be perfect but afterwards I didn't care about the cake. I didn't care if we didn't have desserts. I just wanted everyone to be there.'

'It made it more special,' says Chris, who had to borrow a suit for the wedding because his suit was lost in the earthquake.

Emma is uncomfortable with the symbolism her wedding gained in the aftermath of the earthquake. 'To be honest, I didn't think of anybody else when I was doing the wedding. We just wanted to get married to each other. It never crossed my mind these people who have lost family members are not going to like that because I did not think we were going to be in the limelight.'

Chris says the wedding was a bit unreal but it also allowed them to see the best side of people. A man in Nebraska sent a dollar for a new cake and an American senator's wife sent a moving letter.

'I was on the stretcher and I assumed we wouldn't be getting married and Dad and Chris said, "Yes you are."'

Although the celebrity could be painful, it did have its rewards. They were recognised by the crew on the aircraft to Rarotonga, where they went for their honeymoon, and received free food and a bottle of champagne. The story had gone international and while in Rarotonga they received a call from CBS in New York about an interview. Negotiations proceeded and after their honeymoon the couple were flown to a very cold New York to stay in a luxury hotel five minutes from Central Park. A waiter recognised Chris from the news coverage and gave them free drinks.

Then it was back to Christchurch and reality. One of Emma's first engagements was the funeral of Philip McDonald. Her firm relocated to a single-storey building in Riccarton and Emma says she will never work in a multi-level building again. 'I don't want to be in anything that looks heavy. I cancelled my gym membership because the building it is in looks so heavy. When we had a [magnitude] 5.3 on Saturday, I didn't stop shaking for two hours.'

She goes to counselling once a week and finds it therapeutic to talk about her anxiety and her experience. What she finds most unnerving is what is around the corner. 'The Japan thing [Sendai tsunami in March 2011] affected me quite badly. I like to see what is going on and I like to be informed. It's more what might come. All these disasters, here and overseas. Chris is good at talking me through it, but it's just all happening at once. I don't feel that lucky. I thought [when in the building] I can't be that lucky. I feel it's too good to be true. Sleep is patchy. I lie awake at night and think of what could happen. I can't switch off.'

The experience has not changed Emma's attitude to life, however, and she is looking forward to the future with rock-solid Chris. 'My feelings were already as strong as they could be. I thought my stress levels were going to go out the window. But that lasted about a week. Now I have got new anxiety issues. We were so lucky. Now I take my phone everywhere. In the loo. Everywhere.'

FOOTNOTE: Stage 1 of the Expert Panel Report into the collapse of the PGC building (designed in 1963), released on 30 September 2011, found the cause to be the failure of the reinforced-concrete walls of the core of the structure between Level 1 and Level 2. Subsequently the perimeter columns, and/or joints between the columns, and the beams and the connections between the floor slabs and the shear-core failed, causing the floors to collapse.

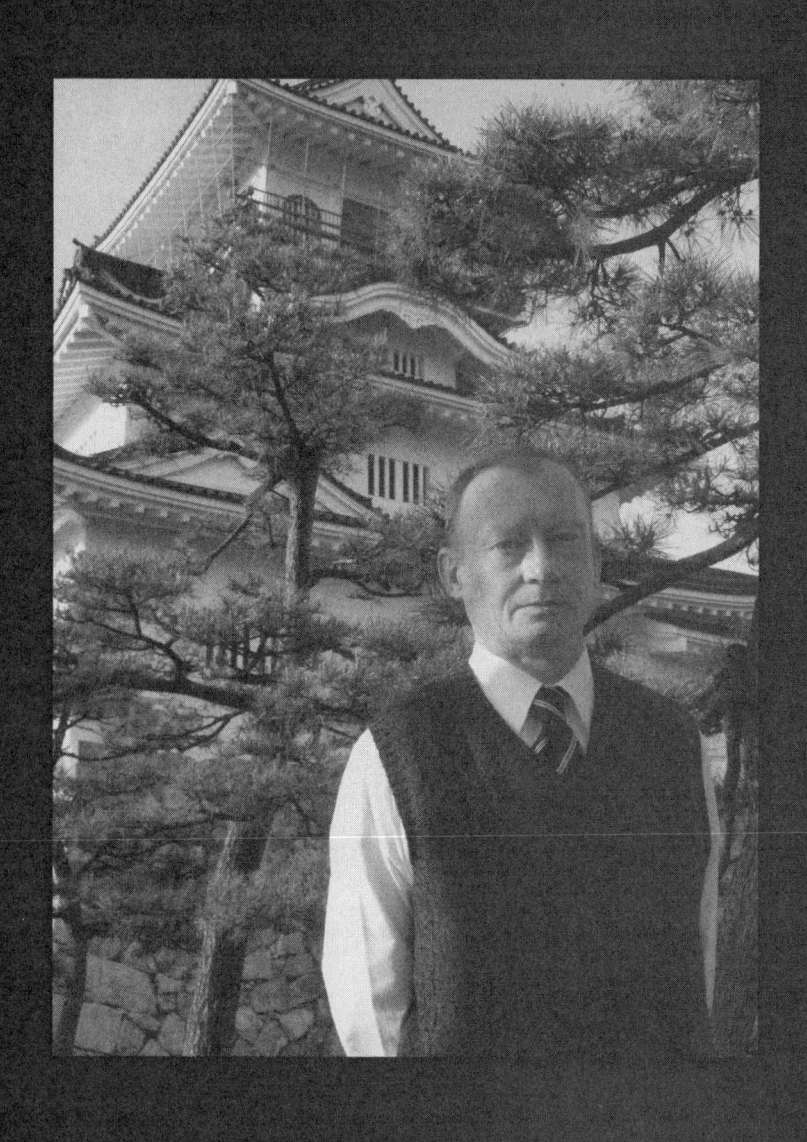

5

DAVID HORSLEY

'I had a very definite feeling of forty-nine years on the planet and felt it was a significant amount of life.'

DAVID HORSLEY IS grateful to have survived the collapse of the CTV building and, perhaps surprisingly, he is also almost grateful for being in the building when it tumbled. The English-language teacher, who was brought up in Tauranga, had accompanied 21 students from the Toyama College of Foreign Languages (TCFL) to Christchurch for a three-week English-immersion experience. Twelve of his students died when the building imploded in the earthquake.

'In some ways I was glad I was in the building. It would have been much harder to face the parents if I had been out having a coffee. As a New Zealander you feel sort of responsible for what happens in your own country,' he says, when interviewed in Toyama in June. 'I do feel some guilt, especially since it is New Zealand. These things don't happen here. You bring them to your own country and you want to show off. It's not part of the plan.'

David was born in Malaysia and came to New Zealand with his family when he was 10. He has a master's in History from Canterbury University and has lived in Toyama since 1987, teaching at the TCFL for about four years. He is separated from his Japanese wife who lives in Tauranga with their two boys, aged 17 and 18.

The trip to Christchurch was always a highlight of the year and he was happy with the cheerful, hardworking group he would be supervising on the trip. The students were always well behaved, he says. 'It's very hard to make them speak English and naturally they revert to Japanese even when they are at the school. This group, however, was trying to speak English before they went and that was good to see.'

His job on such trips was to act as liaison person for the

students, particularly if issues arose with the homestay families. He believes most students were aware of the September earthquake in Christchurch and the college had checked with King's Education that it was safe to come. He helped the students get acquainted with their homestay families after the group arrived on Saturday 19 February, and then he and the other teacher with the group, Tomoko Kiyu, had the rest of the weekend off.

As he walked to King's Education on the morning of the earthquake, it was raining and he made a mental note to get himself an umbrella. He and Tomoko were not needed in the morning, which was an orientation day, and they went out for a coffee in town but were back for lunchtime in the cafeteria. Just before 12.50 p.m. he met up with King's Education teacher Ron Godkin, who had offered to show him where to buy a cheap umbrella. Ron was also originally from Tauranga and had gone to school with David's brother Michael. They headed off to the lift and as they were waiting the building started to shake and roll.

'There was a violent shake and I heard the girls scream. I knew what was happening and it was an aftershock. Then the shaking got more violent and Ron fell down, having lost his balance, and things fell off the wall. I thought, *This is not good*. I might have put a hand on the wall as it shook. It literally came apart, with everything falling and everything coming apart at the seams. I knew very clearly that I was going to die and I thought, *This is the end, this is it*. It's interesting to look back. I was just sure this was it. I had a very definite feeling of forty-nine years on the planet and felt it was a significant amount of life. Things started to fall on my head and I crouched down and put hands over my head.

'We fell but I have no recollection of falling. I closed my eyes and when I opened them I was covered by the dust of the rubble. Ron was lying beside me and we were on a mountain of rubble. I think the floors must have fallen away from us. I can't recall feeling relieved that I was alive. The magnitude of what had happened, the fact the building had come down, really knocked me off centre in terms of what the world should be like. It knocks you sideways. Ron was conscious and covered in dust, his left foot stuck in rubble up to his ankle and he was in great pain.'

David's foot was also stuck and he pulled his foot out of his shoe and then removed his shoe from the rubble. A policeman was climbing up the pile and helped Ron to street level while David, who had cuts to his head but was otherwise uninjured, made his own way down.

'I might have put a hand on the wall as it shook. It literally came apart, with everything falling and everything coming apart at the seams. I knew very clearly that I was going to die . . .'

'A whole mass of people was moving into Latimer Square and almost without thinking we moved to Latimer Square as well. I knew that I had students there and knew Tomoko was there but I knew there was nothing I could do and I was bleeding from cuts to my head.'

He was taken to a medical centre and after having the cuts to his head stitched he tried to get back to the CTV building. 'By the time I was back, a police cordon was up. I texted the school but they had already been contacted by Tomoko, and the school knew people were trapped in the building. Some firemen were at the cordon and they told me that people were alive in the building. I was surprised people had survived because I had an inkling all had died. But to hear they were alive was great. It became a question of how many and how badly they were injured. The fact that we could get some out, and maybe all, was the big hope at that point.'

He returned to Latimer Square where medical staff were treating the injured and prioritising the worst. He tried to find King's Education students who were not in the building at the time of the earthquake. The Japanese consul, Shoichi Kawai, who had been trapped in the Forsyth Barr building on the corner of Armagh and Colombo Streets, had also arrived. David was allowed back to the site at one stage to point to where he believed the searchers should be looking.

About 4 p.m. some of the students started arriving at the triage station and he recognised two of his students who had been sitting closest to the outside wall of the cafeteria. They were both in a reasonable physical state. As he waited in the increasingly cooler late afternoon, he answered a request for a Japanese speaker.

'A short way into triage there was a girl covered in dust and a thermal blanket. She was shivering in shock and had an oxygen mask on. She could only say, "Left leg badly hurt." I lifted her mask and saw it was Norika (Masutani). Her eyes were closed and I thought this is a girl who is close to death. Then they brought in Tomoko. She was coherent and conscious. She was a star, considering all she had been through. She was on the ball. She had injured fingers and she went off to get treatment. She was brilliant, especially considering she was operating in a second language. Things were changing and there was a lot of incorrect information. It was very difficult to find who was out and what condition they were in and where they had been taken.'

He and Tomoko spent the night at a welfare centre set up at Burnside High School, which had power and water.

'I was very worried . . . I knew parents were upset that only the CTV building had gone down in that area, that something had gone wrong and it needed to be explained.'

The next few days were full of confusion and building frustration. There was a rumour about that student Yoshiko Hirauchi, a retired school teacher, had survived and been flown to Auckland for treatment. When senior TCFL teacher Susan Urakami arrived in New Zealand from Toyama she immediately went to Auckland to check the hospitals, but without success. In fact, Yoshiko had died in the building next to her best friend, Hiroko Sato, and her body had been taken to the Burnham Army camp for formal identification.

David says the parents of missing or injured students began arriving in 'dribs and drabs' and were obviously very distraught and stressed. They were also hounded by the Japanese media and their mood was not improved by a bus trip organised, it seems, by the Japanese embassy to view the CTV building. The bus was stopped by officials and David remembers two fathers sprinting towards the building anyway. Eventually the trip was approved and David says the parents were astounded by the difference between the ruined CTV building and other surrounding buildings which had remained standing.

'It was very important for them to see the building. In a sense it did not matter, but they wanted to see the building and what kind of condition it was in. When they did get there, they asked, "Why is the IRD building [opposite the CTV building] not broken? Why are all these other new buildings unscathed?" They felt something was wrong here. If the whole area was a war zone then they could say this is a terrible thing. The parents wanted someone to be found responsible. A person. In Japan someone would bow down and ask forgiveness.'

Other frustrations were the delay in identifying the bodies and last-minute changes to arrangements made after a great deal of organisation. 'We thought we could go and collect the belongings of the dead students but they wanted fingerprints and did not want the belongings to be touched until they had them. It was very, very wrenching. Very, very difficult.'

He returned to Japan on the flight originally booked for the whole group. 'I didn't know what I was going to come back to. I was very worried. I knew I didn't cause the earthquake and did not cause the CTV building to fall down. I knew parents were upset that only the CTV building had gone down in that area, that something had gone wrong and it needed to be explained. They also knew about the earthquake in September. But the parents were tremendously kind to me. They have rallied to support me. They have lost their child but they would come to me and say, "How is your head?"'

He has no sleeping problems or flashbacks but thinks about the ordeal every day.

'When I came back I went to twelve funerals. I arrived back on Sunday morning and went to my first funeral on Sunday night. It hasn't shaken my fundamental beliefs. I am a Christian and it hasn't changed my thinking too much. I remember looking at the Sendai earthquake and tsunami on the way back to Japan when I stayed in Auckland overnight. I have been on a camping trip right through that area. You can plan your life as much as you like but this sort of thing happens. Perhaps it's better to try and have some goals but not to think that is what is going to happen.'

> **'When I came back I went to twelve funerals.'**

'The thing I thought about most was, *Did I do the best I could have done?* When I came down from the CTV building, people were going to Latimer Square and I went too. Why did I do that? I knew people were in the building. My students. Why didn't I say I'm going to look for my students? Did I really do the best I could do? You are transported to this other world and how do you react without training or experience? I wouldn't say I kick myself. If you think about it too much, you go a bit crazy.'

He says he wants to continue teaching at the school and is committed to staying in Japan. The school, he believes, is in good heart and the survivors who have returned to resume their courses are 'getting on with it'. This year's intake has been similar to previous years', dispelling fears the school would be tainted, he adds.

'Japanese people will always surprise. They [the surviving students] don't hang out as the earthquake survivor group. They are very resilient.'

Above: Workers being lowered by rope from the Forsyth Barr building. JOHN KIRK-ANDERSON, *THE PRESS*

Right: Rescuers at work on the Pyne Gould Corporation building.

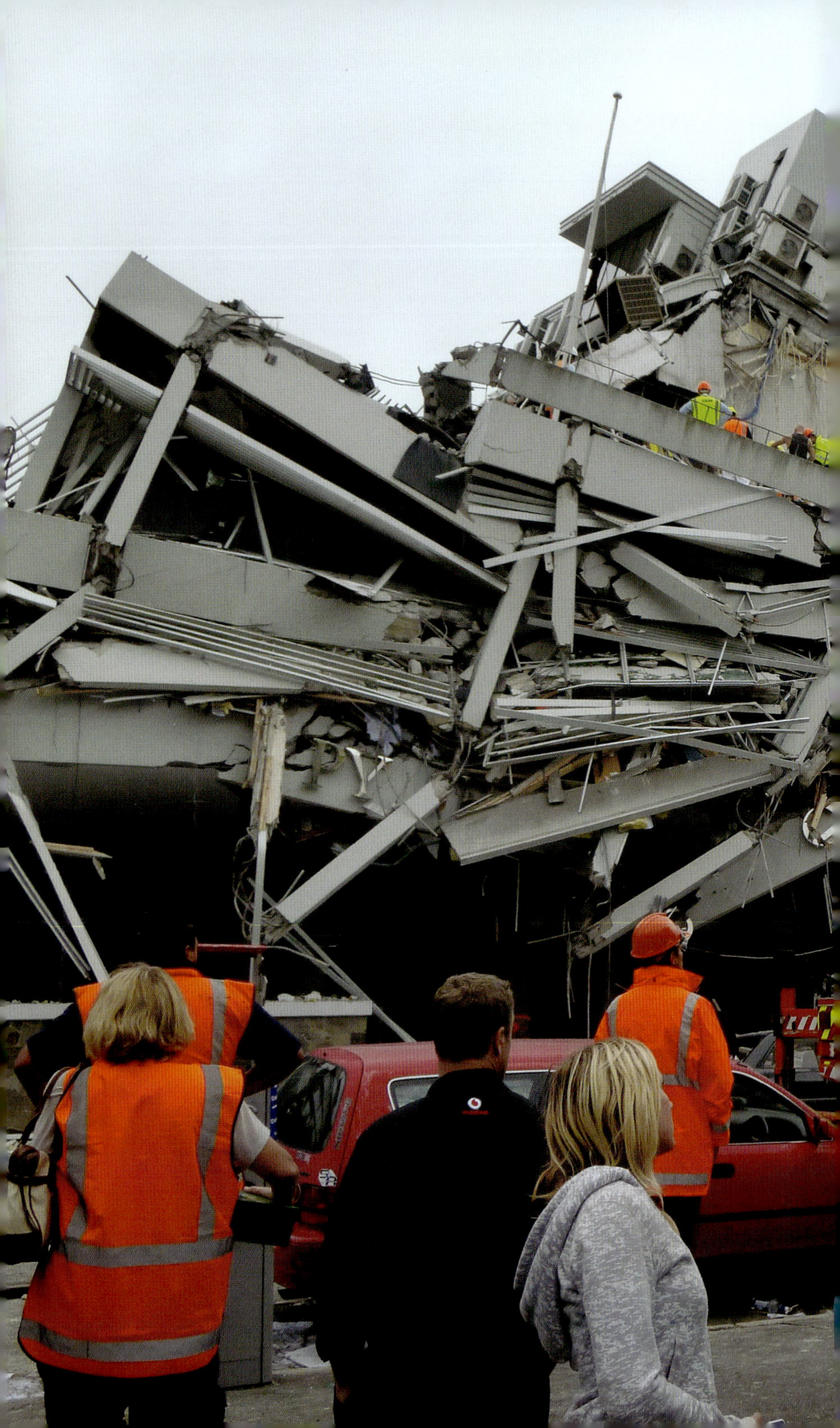

Rescuers and colleagues outside the Pyne Gould Corporation building in Cambridge Terrace on the afternoon of the earthquake.

Photos taken by Emma Greenslade as she was trapped in the PGC building, showing the surroundings of her concrete prison. EMMA GREENSLADE

From left: Emma Service, Matt Parkin and Bonnie Singh.

6

EMMA SERVICE
BONNIE SINGH
MATT PARKIN

'I felt the bricks coming down behind me and they were getting my legs and that's when I screamed.'

ON 22 FEBRUARY 2011, the crew at Southern Ink tattoo studio were getting ready to ink one of their own. The owner, Matt Parkin, a self-taught tattoo artist of 20-years standing, was getting his gear ready to tattoo his assistant Emma Service. She had designed a 'sleeve' for her left arm and since it was quiet Matt had time to do the tattoo.

The studio was in an old part of Colombo Street between Tuam and St Asaph Streets, with the Adam and Eve adult supplies shop on one side and the Lotus Heart restaurant, run by devotees of the Indian guru Sri Chinmoy, on the other. Southern Ink had its premises at street level and the floor above was empty.

His anxiety about the building prompted an exit plan, which was to get out of the building and onto the street as soon as a shake struck.

After the September earthquake the old brick building, owned offshore, was green-stickered, which meant it had been inspected and was considered safe for use. But Matt says he never felt the same about it. Big chunks of plaster had fallen from the ceiling and in almost every aftershock white dust would drift down, covering the studio. His anxiety about the building prompted an exit plan, which was to get out of the building and onto the street as soon as a shake struck. An alternative route was out the back of the shop and down an alleyway but Matt thought that too dangerous because of high brick walls on all sides. 'I was always uneasy in that building but I don't like earthquakes anyway. It was always on my mind that something might happen and I wanted to be prepared,' Matt says.

Bonnie Singh had started her day at the shop about 10.30 a.m. and was greeted by Matt's apprentice Matti McEachen, who called Matt the 'Jedi master'. A graphic designer and rock band member, Matti was a talented salesman and had a warm, friendly and positive manner with people. Two days before he died, the passionate tattoo artist had tattooed a large koi fish on his thigh.

'Hey buddy,' he said to Bonnie. It was her fifth week at the studio and her second week full-time. She had left her previous job as cash controller for Pak'nSave, because she loved drawing and wanted to learn how to tattoo. 'I was singing as usual and Matti put on a song that he said was his favourite love song. Then he played mine on the computer.'

Emma arrived with her partner Shannon and 16-month-old baby Ella (she also has a three-year-old) and they chatted until Matt arrived. Both Bonnie and Matti were wearing new footwear and they had a laugh about Matt complimenting Bonnie on her new 'Demonias' and Matti, who was wearing new high-sided Puma boots, thinking he was the target of the flattery.

'Matti was helping me out and we got to sizing Em's tattoo,' Matt says. 'We had a chat about doing some self-portraits and Matti looked at me, listening intently, with a half-smile on his face, just like he always did. He was genuinely interested in anything anybody had to say. He was working on his Sir Ed portrait which was looking real good. Then he began finalising the stencil with Em. Everything was ready to go, ink caps poured, everything wrapped, machines set.'

Needing a pause, Matt went into the alleyway behind the shop and Emma came out to have a smoke with him. Matt says the earthquake that struck at 12.51 p.m. nearly knocked him over. His first thought was to run out onto Colombo Street through the shop, but he headed down the alleyway behind the shop instead. Emma was in front of him. 'As we headed for the corner and into the alleyway the whole back block of the shop we referred to as "the ghetto" fell down, causing a huge dust cloud of cement and a horrible noise. Em disappeared in the cloud of dust and I thought, *She's gone*. I looked up and everything was still shaking like mad. I knew I had to get away from all the bricks.'

Emma says the quake started as a low rumble and she saw Matt bolting and followed his lead. 'Matt disappeared and I kind of froze. Something was telling me not to run and I just stood and put my hands over my head. I felt the bricks coming down behind me and they were getting my legs and that's when I screamed. I closed my eyes and then it stopped and it was just white and I couldn't see a thing. I heard Matt calling out for me and I thought, *Thank f—k, he is OK.*'

Incredibly, one potentially lethal wall of the ghetto had stayed up. With his heart thumping, Matt leapt onto the stairs leading to the Lotus Heart's back courtyard and jumped on a table, smashing it flat.

'There was dust everywhere and I didn't know where to go. That's when it stopped shaking. I looked around and saw Em coming out of the dust by the stairs I had just gone up. She had been hit by falling bricks but was OK.'

They went into the Lotus Heart kitchen and saw the front of the restaurant had caved in. Reluctant to carry on through the Lotus Heart to Colombo Street, they decided to try the alleyway again. It was now piled high with fallen bricks. Matt tried the back door of the studio but it was jammed shut and he got no response when he called out Bonnie's and Matti's names.

'When we made it onto Colombo Street, I couldn't believe the damage,' Matt says. 'The front of the shop was gone; it was just covered in rubble. It was surreal that so much damage could happen in what felt like ten seconds. The whole front and sides of the ghetto upstairs above our shop had fallen off and onto the veranda and crushed it down onto the pavement. I was yelling "Matti" because there were a lot of people around and he may have been among them.

'Then I looked where the front door would have been and I saw Matti's legs with the jeans and new shoes I had seen him wearing just minutes ago. The amount of debris on him was incredible. There was no way I thought he could be alive under there and he wasn't moving when I yelled his name.

'Em and I broke down once we knew it was him. I couldn't even stand up, my legs weren't working. I went into shock. I sat down. Just then we heard Bonnie yelling out for Matti as she climbed out over the debris, out a little hole where the front door used to be.'

Emma says she just couldn't believe what had happened and went into denial. She took some of the bricks off Matti but could not do it for long. 'I remember the panic and realising what had happened. A random woman helped me to breathe.'

Shortly before the shaking started Bonnie had been helping two young American women, Rachel Conley and Jackie Kinder (Chapter 22), sort out a tattoo. Jackie wanted the words 'Let it be' tattooed on the back of her leg and as Matti, who was keen to do the tattoo, was busy with Emma, they were given an appointment for later in the day.

'I started sorting out the font for the tattoo when suddenly the shop started shaking,' Bonnie says. 'I just sat on my chair waiting for it to stop. Matti came over to me, looked at me with a *holy shit* expression on his face. The lights went out and it started shaking more violently, and I saw him turn to run. I scrambled for my phone, jumped up, and followed behind him, just watching his feet and trying hard to maintain my balance.

'I saw Matti reach the sliding door, and was thinking to myself, *Whew, safety*. I saw him reach his arms out, slide the door back and then pause for a couple of seconds to balance in the frame of the door. Then he walked out. All I saw was his shoes disappear. I still thought we were going to be sweet because I was still calm. Earthquakes didn't really worry me.'

Just as she reached the sliding door Bonnie received what felt like a colossal blow to the head and thought she would die. She woke up on the floor covered in boards, bricks and rubble and terrified she would bleed to death before anybody found her.

'I started yelling, "Help me, please!" and I turned and ran to the back door, hunched over from the pain. I tried to open the door but it was jammed. I could hear Matt on the other side trying to open it too. We couldn't hear what each other was saying. I was so terrified of the building blowing over like a deck of cards. It felt so fragile.'

She went back to the front of the shop and in the darkness saw a small gap where the glass frontage used to be. She crawled on top of the rubble and pulled bricks out of the way. 'As I made my way down the bricks on the outside, I noticed Matti was not standing there, and a wave of shock and terror ran through me. I screamed, "Where's Matti? Where's Matti?"'

Matt and Emma gave her a hug and told her Matti was under the rubble. Matt says people came over and started pulling debris off his friend. He did not want to see Matti's crushed body and he and Emma moved away.

> 'Em and I just kept saying to each other, "We made it. We made it out. We are alive." Every time we thought of Matti, we cried.'

'I felt responsible because it was my shop. It was just the last thing I expected to see. I wanted to get away. I hated that building. I didn't know about the others. I thought we got screwed personally. I hated Colombo Street, the ghetto and the aftershocks. We couldn't handle being around any buildings. Em and I just kept saying to each other, "We made it. We made it out. We are alive." Every time we thought of Matti, we cried.'

Bonnie was driven to hospital by a kind stranger who smoked frantically all the way and asked Bonnie about her four-year-old daughter Ebony. As she was driven away, Bonnie saw Matt and Emma sitting on the side of the road holding each other and Jackie Kinder, outside the Lotus Heart, screaming for her friend Rachel. Rachel was killed on the footpath not far from Matti.

Bonnie says she thought Matti would be dug out and he would join her in hospital. She was in so much pain she was having trouble breathing. When she got to hospital she was shaking violently and feeling nauseous. 'I didn't feel relieved at all. I didn't want to die like this. I had come so far and I just wanted to see my baby again. Throughout it all I was trying hard to keep up with all the texts that were coming through on my phone. I didn't want anyone to panic, so I tried to make my replies seem normal. I tried to be brave and strong because I knew there was a chance Matti would be brought in, so I needed to be on the lookout for him.'

In the increasing chaos of the hospital with people running and yelling she was placed in a corner, in a dark room. 'Still scared for my life, I broke down hard and cried aloud. My legs had gone numb. I couldn't feel or move them, and I was alone and scared. A man, a social worker I think, comforted me and gave me some water.'

She finally saw a doctor who declared her OK although she certainly didn't feel it. She was told to ring her husband Daniel to pick her up but was still reluctant to leave in case Matti turned up. 'Every bed and wheelchair that came past got my heart racing. *Will this be Matti?* It's what kept me going that day. The thought of him coming in in a wheelchair, broken but alive, and smiling. I imagined we would share a room, and make fun of each other and whinge about who was hurt the most. It's amazing the strength that hope has. I needed to believe he was going to be OK to make it through that day.'

'Still scared for my life, I broke down hard and cried aloud. My legs had gone numb. I couldn't feel or move them, and I was alone and scared.'

Daniel arrived, to her great relief, and she broke down again. After another doctor examined her, she was put in a hard neck brace and wheeled into a ward filled with other victims, including Glenn Prattley (Chapter 18), who had a badly broken leg, and had lost his five-week-old baby and partner. 'His screams were so haunting. He was yelling, "Cut both my legs off. I need to find my baby." He pleaded with the nurses to let him go, so he could dig his family from the rubble. I have never heard such pain and sadness in someone's voice. My heart sank.'

X-rays showed she had five fractures in her spine and two in her neck. She needed to stay on her back until a brace could be sent up from Dunedin.

About 9 p.m. a social worker told her Matti had died in Colombo Street. 'My world fell apart. I just kept saying, "Oh no, oh please no," just like in the movies. This was the worst moment of my life. After that moment, I was in a dark place for days just wanting to close my eyes and slip away.'

All Emma and Matt wanted to do was find their families and hug them. They went to a friend's house and borrowed a scooter which turned out to be a godsend, given the parlous state of the roads. Matt dropped Emma at her daughter's pre-school before heading home to Burwood. After a tortuous trip through cracked, flooded and bumpy streets, sticky with wet sand, Matt picked up his son, Seth, from pre-school and rode through the broken suburbs to home where, nearly six hours after the walls fell and Matti died, he hugged his partner Jak.

In early June, Matt says he still struggles with the aftershocks and is angry the verandas outside his shop and others were not propped up after the September earthquake. He says the danger was evident and many deaths could have been prevented. 'It's just ridiculous, mate. To have a wake-up call like September and not prop up those verandas. It was crazy. They are all propped up in Riccarton now. They had no support or pillars holding them up.'

Bonnie says at first she felt guilty for being alive. 'I didn't think I deserved to be. I mean, my life was in no way as important as Matti's, was what I kept thinking. I thought about how his family must hate me for breathing, for still being here. I thought about how his hundreds of friends were going to resent me. I just felt guilt all the time, and self-ishly never thought about my own family, and how they would feel if it was me who had died. How my daughter would have no mother. Instead I just thought about how I was feeling and let it consume me.'

Four months after Matti's death, Bonnie's back is still sore. She says she still feels a bit numb about the experience, not seeing it as quite real. 'Each day it becomes a bit clearer. I have moved on from feeling guilty. I have a lot to do with Matti's family and have met all his friends. Mentally I know what I have to go through. Hanging out with people, drawing, painting; it all helps.'

Emma says she doesn't take a day for granted.

'Live it like you could be gone tomorrow,' says Matt. 'It's a big change for me. I always thought like that but didn't really act on it. I always cherished the days but this is a big wake-up call to practise it rather than just think about it nicely.'

All three are hesitant about going to town and don't even like going to the supermarket. They avoid malls and feel very protective of their children. Wherever Matt goes, he looks for the earthquake triangle and in the supermarket looks for the biggest freezer. Bonnie has a mental checklist. 'Where not to stand. Where not to walk. Where is the safest place to go.'

It was a couple of months before Matt was ready to tattoo again. His first was the tattoo Emma had wanted on her arm. He is now working from home and is thankful to the tattooing community for replacing his lost equipment. 'We will get another shop. It won't have anything on top of it. It will be somewhere like Hornby.'

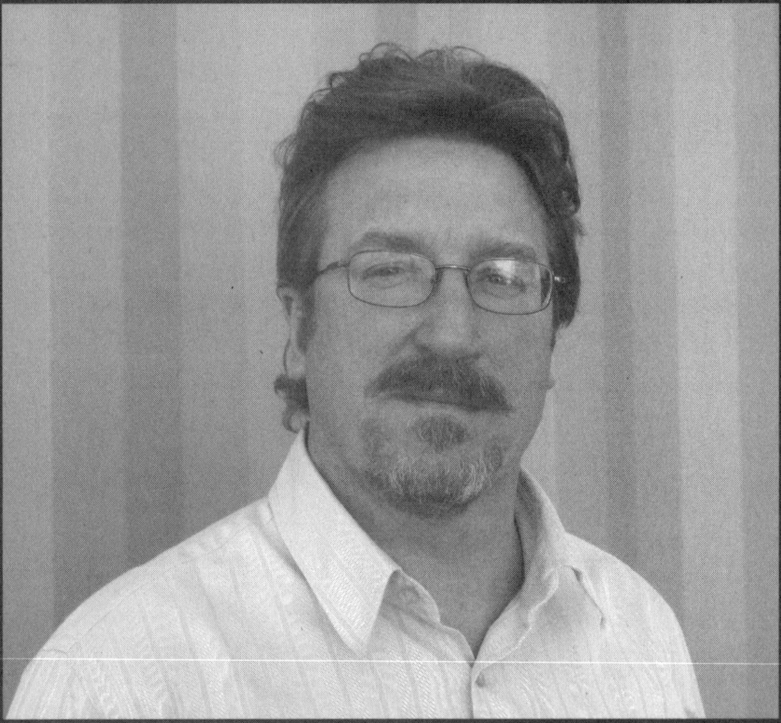

7

TIM CRONSHAW

'There's no good reason why I'm alive today.
By all the odds I should be dead.'

TRAPPED, CLAUSTROPHOBIC AND thinking he was going to die, it could not have been much worse for *The Press* farm reporter Tim Cronshaw. But perhaps there was a glimmer of hope. He started kicking, forcing his way out of the rubble on top of him. Then there was fresh air, and it never felt so good.

Only minutes before Tim was having lunch. Being a creature of habit he likes to take a proper break between 12.30 and 1.30 p.m. On 22 February, the habit took him up to the *Press* cafeteria, a floor up from the newsroom, for a toasted sandwich, and very nearly his death. At 12.51 p.m., when Christchurch was shaken by the 6.3 magnitude earthquake centred at the head of the Heathcote Valley, about 10 km east of the *Press*, he was in the most vulnerable part of the celebrated 102-year-old building.

Tim, who had been at *The Press* since 2004, had just finished his toasted sandwiches and his apple when the earthquake began to shake the building. 'I thought it was just another aftershock but it soon became apparent it was a bit more than that. I headed to one of the cast iron pillars, thinking that was the place to be and for a start it was. Then the whole building was groaning and creaking and things started caving in.'

Lyn Reid (Chapter 16), one of the *Press*'s two housekeepers, who was also on her lunch break and sitting at a table next to Tim, grabbed his shirt and Tim managed to get them both to the apparent safety of the pillar. Then it started leaning alarmingly and snapped off at floor level. 'The forces to do that were just incredible,' Tim says.

The forces were also doing terrible damage to the internal brick cafeteria wall which held up the beams and roof. The roof was flat and made of solid concrete and steel. It was designed to enable more levels to be built in the future and had in the past hosted the odd staff party.

> '**I dived towards the stairwell and the whole thing caved in and I thought, *I am dead*. I absolutely thought I was dead.**'

'I lunged forward and tried to get to my feet. Then the concrete beam came down on my shoulder. I had several options and only a split second to choose. I dived towards the stairwell and the whole thing caved in and I thought, *I am dead*. I absolutely thought I was dead.

'Everything went black. There was dust everywhere, the noise was amazing and I suddenly realised I was alive. But unfortunately for me it was worse, because I'm claustrophobic and I was stuck in this mini-cavern which wasn't much bigger than me, stretched out on my stomach.'

At 1.9 metres tall and weighting 110 kg, Tim has the stature and body mass of an All Black lock, so the space confining him would probably have housed two smaller people. 'I started yelling for help and heard Lyn yelling too. A concrete beam had come down on both her legs. It seemed there was nothing I could do. I was freaking out.'

A steel girder separated them and in the darkness he felt the blood coming from a cut in his head but realised the wound wasn't serious. 'Then there was a little bit of light at my feet and that was a huge thing for me because it soon became obvious no-one was going to help us for some time. I found my glasses and cleaned them up. I talked to Lyn. She was in incredible pain at that stage. I started kicking away rubble with my feet.'

His kicking slowly pushed back the rubble and he managed to squeeze his way out beneath the steel beam. 'It was the best feeling in my life to be out in the fresh air and I looked down and saw Lyn and thought, *Oh Jesus, this poor lady is pinned, just absolutely trapped*. She was saying, "Get me out. I want to get off this building." So, stupidly in hindsight, I tried to pull [the beam] up but there was no way and all I could do was console her and tell her we had survived and everything else was secondary and just be patient because help would come.' He promised not to leave her.

In the fresh air he was able to look around and see the carnage not only close to him but around the city. He looked over to Christchurch Cathedral and saw its spire had crashed to the ground. He could hear voices coming from the collapsed area next to the cafeteria, the location of the *Press*'s finance division, where administrator Adrienne Lindsay, 54, lost her life.

Several other *Press* staff were also trapped in the cafeteria not far from Tim. It could have been much worse, because normally the cafeteria would have been much busier at the time the earthquake hit.

'One of the first guys to come up was George Piper (the *Press* in-house builder and fixer) and he was amazing. He put his life on the line. He realised the building could collapse at any stage after every aftershock and that was my thought as well. The building was going down.'

Together, Tim and George used bits of concrete to prop up the beam trapping Lyn to ensure it didn't exert any more pressure in an aftershock. George then went back downstairs to turn off an emergency generator. He returned to pull doors and rubble off digital technician Bruce King, who was trapped with a crushed foot just outside the cafeteria door.

'Then a series of aftershocks shook the building and I had to fight every survival instinct not to get off [the building]. A promise was a promise. I was desperate to find out if my family had survived, and was worried particularly for my son, who was at a school with vulnerable 100-year-old buildings. The cellphone coverage was down but I rattled out text messages anyway. I had to fight tears when the first ones came through and they were all safe.'

Construction workers from the building company Ganellen, who had been working on a new seven-storey building into which the

Press was to move in the next few weeks, also arrived, having negotiated the gap between the new and old buildings. The new building, built on the former *Press* printing works site, was to the north-east of the old *Press* building and was only a jump away from the cafeteria.

Lyn was still trapped. An engineer arrived with a hydraulic jack and tried to lift the beam trapping her but the floor under the jack began to collapse. Two doctors had come and after checking Lyn went to minister to the trapped finance section staff. With numerous emergency staff now on the roof it was suggested that Tim, who had been on the roof for over two hours, should leave.

'Urban rescue experts came with specialist lifting gear. One told me it was time to get off the building. I told him I wouldn't go without Lyn. He said she was under good care and insisted I leave. It seemed to make sense so I said goodbye to Lyn and left with one of the Ganellen builders. I don't know how she managed the pain.

'Nervously, we bridged the gap between the buildings with the ground many floors below and then the second-largest aftershock hit. I turned around to see more parts of the cafeteria collapse and the rescue workers being shoved around as if they were on a giant trampoline. I thought they were all goners. The new building felt as if it was going down too and we sprinted through darkened stairways and down a ramp into Gloucester Street. It was only then, when I saw all the buildings down and turned around the corner to see the broken cathedral and, behind me, cars caved in by collapsed shops, that I realised many more people were less lucky than me.'

Tim got home under his own steam, driving through broken and holed streets. His wife Tina was just about to bike into town with her neighbour to look for him. When he saw Tina, the bottled up shock and emotion burst through and he broke down.

Tim dismisses talk of heroics. 'Lyn would have done the same. I think you just do those things. Lots of people were heroes that day. It was just something you do to help out. There's no good reason why I'm alive today. By all the odds I should be dead.'

Today he continues in his job as *The Press* farming reporter. While some of the effects of the experience have worn off, he thinks about it every day and how it could have ended very differently. 'As time has passed I have coped better with the backwash of emotions which follow when a building caves in on you. It's helped that I'm not a high–low person. I've been lucky enough to never get depressed about bad points in my life and believe in the character trait of toughing out the bad times. I declined every offer afterwards of counselling. I guess that's because I wanted to deal with it in my own way.

'The way I have dealt with it is to treat the whole event like a book. Every so often I open this book in my mind, dip into a few pages, think about what happened and close the book. That works best for me.'

Tim says the first few nights after the earthquake were the worst, not just because of the aches, pains, grazes and bruises. He was unable to help the family put up tents in the backyard. The mental strain of that first night stays with him.

'I've always been a great sleeper and struggled to doze off initially because of the pain in my shoulders and neck. Then images of the roof collapsing played over and over in my mind. The worst flashbacks were of being trapped. I replayed my actions and was constantly irritated with myself for not moving left to the kitchenette where I could have got Lyn and myself to complete safety.

'I felt guilty that I stayed up on the building with Lyn rather than getting down to look after my own wife and family, even though text messages confirmed they were safe. I felt guilty that I did not do enough on that upper floor to help out other people.

'The great thing about the human spirit is that we are internally wired to survive and make the most of life. I don't know if the earthquake has changed my life. It probably has. Knowing you had a narrow escape from death makes you appreciate your family and friends and the small things in life. My wife and I are probably living for the day a bit more, instead of always saving for the future, but this was something we had been working on for the last few years anyway. I do know that I take less crap from people. I suppose if your life is short why should you?'

He used to think his fitness and background in competitive sport might have helped him to survive but no longer thinks so. 'People died that day despite not panicking and making every right move. Others were gripped by fear or panicked and ran into danger and survived. Too often it was simply about being in the right or wrong place at the right or wrong time.'

FOOTNOTE: The *Press* building has now been demolished. It consisted of a historic heritage section and a large, two-storey add-on. The historic section was finished in 1909 when *The Press* moved to its grand new home from premises in Cashel Street. The new site contained the new Collins and Harman-designed office building and a new printing works. The first newspaper produced from the building rolled from the presses on 22 February 1909. The date, discovered anew after the 22 February earthquake, had an obvious resonance for *Press* staff.

In many ways the building was a marvel of engineering for its time. The Gothic-style edifice, with its Oamaru stone exterior was the first ferro-concrete building in Christchurch and featured steel girders and stout brick walls. It was regarded as almost fireproof and the printing works was equipped with the latest rotary presses. Later earthquake-strengthening made the building stronger.

The building was bought by Australian property and construction company Ganellen in 2010. Its engineers declared the building safe after repairs were needed following the September earthquake and the Boxing Day aftershocks. *The Press* commissioned its own engineer's reports as well. Both views were that the building was safe for use.

Ann Bodkin with partner Graham Richardson.

8

ANN BODKIN

'When the sounds came close to me, I worried they might drill through me as well as the concrete. But when the sounds went away, I worried they weren't coming back.'

WITH A PIECE of broken perspex Ann Bodkin, a claustrophobic, tapped her way around the lightless cavity in which she was trapped. Apart from the underside of her crushed desk, it was concrete. *A concrete coffin*, she thought.

In the next 26 hours her cramped concrete coffin in the Pyne Gould Corporation building in Cambridge Terrace became cold and then wet as the building's fire sprinklers intermittently came on and off. At the end of those 26 hours, she emerged into the bright sun of a new day, relatively unscathed, the last survivor of the 22 February earthquake to be rescued.

Ann worked on the third level of the ordinary 1960s building as a team leader for the Education Review Office, a school inspectorate which is part of the Ministry of Education. After growing up in Southland where her father was a school teacher, she trained as a primary school teacher, later gaining master's degrees in Education and Business Administration. Her desk was in the south-east corner of the building, from where she looked out on the tree-lined banks of the Avon River.

The four-level PGC building had no particular worries for Ann after the earthquake on 4 September although she and co-workers pressured the landlord to change the heavy plaster ceiling tiles above their desks to lighter 'pinex' tiles. On 22 February she spent the morning at her desk and thought about going for a walk at lunchtime but decided to rest a sore foot. At 12.44 p.m. she sent an email to her partner of 11 years, Manchester-born Graham Richardson.

Only five minutes later she heard a huge roar and the building started to shake violently. 'I knew straight away this was no ordinary aftershock and was up out of my chair and under my desk in no time.'

Before she had got very far she was hit by a ceiling tile and then much harder on her back and shoulder, leaving her sprawled flat on the floor on her front. 'It was all so sudden. Twenty seconds and then silence. I started calling out "Can anyone hear me?", but there was nothing but silence. Soon alarms and sirens were wailing and a fire engine arrived right outside the corner of the building where I was trapped. Help was at hand but at the same time I thought the building must be in bad shape.'

Fortunately, unlike some of her fellow captives in the wrecked building, Ann could see a hint of daylight through a small opening in the wreckage, but it wasn't enough to light the space she was trapped in. Luckily, no part of her body was pinned and she could move around slightly, to her left and right, and could also move herself off the floor. She found the piece of perspex and used it to explore her cavern. Above her was the underside of the crushed desk but everything else seemed to be concrete. The floor on which she lay was also on a slope which ended with a 25 metre drop. And she was alone. About five or six workmates were also caught in the building but they were rescued within an hour and Ann did not see or hear them.

'Over the next few hours I heard hysterical sobbing and people clapping as others were rescued. I could hear engines, drilling and what sounded like sledgehammers. When the sounds came close to me, I worried they might drill through me as well as the concrete. But when the sounds went away, I worried they weren't coming back.

'I am claustrophobic and that is why I always took the stairs. I very rarely took the lift. I am not good in small spaces. But I was so focused on the fact that I was alive and I had some air to breathe that I didn't feel too bad. I was just focused on getting out.'

Her determination to survive the ordeal was fuelled by thoughts of her ageing parents. Bill, 80, and Shirley, 79, who still live in Southland, had visited her at work a few weeks before the earthquake and their first thought on 22 February was that Ann would be fine as she worked in a nice modern building. In 1999, her 41-year-old brother Ross, a mine supervisor and father of three children, died in the North Parkes mine accident in New South Wales. Ann had seen the shattering effect Ross's death had had on her parents. 'I said that to my dad afterwards. One of the things that kept me going was that I couldn't let them lose a second child. I knew how devastating it was to lose Ross. One of the things I kept saying was, "I'm not going to let you go through that again, Mum and Dad."'

She continued calling and banging the perspex against a leg of the desk as soon as she thought rescuers might be close and the drilling and banging stopped. No-one heard. As the hours wore on, the reality that she could be trapped overnight prompted her to remove her one contact lens and also to relieve herself. The chasm proved useful for something.

At home in Rolleston, about 20 km south of Christchurch, Graham was understandably worried sick. A neighbour had broken the news the PGC building had collapsed and seeing the wreckage of the building on television coverage, he feared the worst. 'I was in a mess. I couldn't see how anyone could have survived.'

He drove immediately into town and because of the traffic chaos did not get to Hagley Park for three-and-a-half hours. He trekked through the park to the Civil Defence Headquarters at the City Art Gallery and filed a missing person's report. He then headed to Christchurch Hospital in case Ann had been taken there and stayed until 9.30 p.m. when staff told him it was no use waiting. Grief-stricken, he went home for a sleepless night.

Next morning as he made the bed, he broke down completely. 'I thought I could be making the bed for someone who is no longer here. I wanted to hope for the best but of course I was thinking about the worst.'

During the night, conditions for Ann in the concrete coffin became even harder to bear. She could hear drilling nearby and soon water started trickling down on her. 'I had been coping pretty well until then but the sprinklers made me soaking wet. Eventually it stopped but it started again twice when the drilling started. It didn't stop before I was thoroughly drenched and very cold. I started shivering uncontrollably. This time when I needed to relieve myself I couldn't be bothered with all the rigmarole and enjoyed a moment of warmth in the cold.

'About that time a light caught my eye off to my left. I looked over and saw a palm tree shimmering in an area where before there was nothing but concrete. As I watched, the scene changed and I saw people swimming in the sea and island girls dancing on the beach. I realised I was hallucinating and watched with interest. It changed into vivid pink and purple shapes drifting towards me. I turned my head but the shapes stayed. They were pretty and calming so I was just happy to lie there and watch.'

Ann continued to shiver with cold and in response she devised an exercise regime to control it. 'I kept repeating it into the night and next morning. First I wriggled my legs, then rubbed my arms and upper torso. Finally I shuffled over to the edge of the desk where I had a little more height and lifted myself so I could shake my upper body.'

She nearly dozed off several times but she forced herself to stay awake. She was frightened of missing a contact with rescuers and also worried she would succumb to hypothermia. Meanwhile rescuers continued cutting their way into the pancaked building through the night and at last there came what seemed like a breakthrough for Ann.

A man called out to her, 'Is that you, Sean?'

'I said, "No, it's Ann." He called to me again but I realised he had no idea where I was or who I was and probably thought I was one of those people on the second floor that rescuers had already made contact with.'

The coloured shapes and patterns that had continued to appear changed to sinister, black, angry shapes coming from a vivid pink background. 'I told them I didn't want to see them and shut my eyes. I started thinking of the trip Graham and I had taken last year to the

United States, Europe and the UK. I tried to do it in a logical way, starting with getting on the plane. I never got past New Orleans.'

The happy thoughts chased away the black images and then she again made contact with the men working outside. 'They assured me they were working on making the building safer and they would be back to get me at daylight. I was very reassured. Towards morning I realised my Morse code was a little rusty and changed my tapping pattern from OSO to SOS.'

As day broke and work continued, Ann waited patiently for her rescuers but began to realise, as voices moved away from her, that the reassuring exchange she had had earlier had brought rescuers no closer to finding her. 'They obviously had no idea where I was,' Ann says.

That was one of the very few times she despaired, but it was only briefly. 'I would hear people and have hope again. I kept telling myself about the people who had been pulled out of rubble days and days after being trapped, so I knew I had plenty of time and I knew Graham would make sure people would keep looking for me.'

She continued her exercise routine and began to dry out a little. As time dragged on she began to prepare herself mentally for another night in the building. By then it was nearly 11 a.m., 22 hours after the earthquake. 'All of a sudden the machines were turned off and for the first time there was silence. I started banging the perspex against the radiator and calling out but there was only silence. After a while I heard voices and I called out again. I heard a voice saying, "That sounded like a lady's voice."

Simon Bouda, a reporter for the Australian Channel 9 television station, had come to the PGC site to film an urban search and rescue crew from New South Wales. He heard the tapping in the rubble and alerted rescuers, who quickly swung into action and assured her they would get her out. 'For the first time in my concrete coffin I cried,' Ann says. 'I figured some of these guys might know my brother so I started to have that conversation. But every time I talked they had to stop the machinery. I realised they didn't want to talk to me at all.

They were there to focus on getting me out. So I stopped trying to make polite conversation and let them get on with their jobs.'

Graham, who was still at home and about to come into town, got the call soon after. Words can hardly describe how he felt, he says. Tears well up and he looks away. He rushed into town towards the building and although army staff at one road block would not let him through, he took off anyway. 'I didn't think they would shoot me,' he says.

In three hours, with Ann's guidance, the team had removed enough concrete for her to be pulled to safety. She was handed a bottle of water and took a swig although she was never hungry or thirsty during her ordeal. The rescuers told her the cavity in which she was trapped was not nearly as solid as she had thought.

'Just then there was a major aftershock. It was the first time I felt scared. The rescue team stepped up a few gears and within minutes I was blinking in the sunshine as they eased me onto a ladder and down to the ground.'

It was nearly 2.30 p.m., around 26 hours after the earthquake of the previous day.

She was passed through a number of hands and, as Graham recalls, everyone was trying to get them together. 'The sun came out when she came out. It was quite amazing really,' Graham says.

'I heard Graham's voice and it sounded so good,' says Ann, who, with a neck brace on, giggled in response. Graham can't remember what he said, although Ann reckons it was something like, 'Hello, my love.'

Ann was whisked off to the emergency department at Christchurch Hospital, disappointed not to be going home immediately. But despite the elation of her rescue she was suffering dehydration and her heart rate was fluctuating wildly. Graham left the hospital about 9 p.m. to have a drink with friends who had come to support him. Next morning Ann was free to go, thinking there was nothing wrong with her but sore muscles. But the sore muscles persisted and closer inspection over the following days revealed that she had a cracked rib and a broken collarbone.

By June life is returning to a new sort of normal for Ann. She is working from home and has no trouble sleeping or with flashbacks or nightmares, but her back is giving her problems and she continues to suffer headaches from delayed concussion. She does not cope well with confined, windowless spaces and Graham has had to rescue her from Dunedin after an unfortunate reaction to the Southern Cross hotel. 'I couldn't handle that. I thought I was Superwoman. I still go into buildings and think what the best way out is and a lot of my colleagues do the same. I had trouble with my breathing and my doctor suggests it might be something to do with being in enclosed rooms.'

Graham says the feelings aroused over the hours Ann was trapped were not simply forgotten with her rescue. 'I sometimes felt more emotional after the event than during it. I did look to the future without Ann. The adrenalin lasts for a long time. We were in this other world for another month and then started returning to normal.'

Ann struggles to explain her exceptional coping ability under pressure. She says she comes from a family of 'fairly staunch, stroppy women'. Girls in her family could do everything and were expected to. 'All my family are pretty strong. I have a wonderful life. I have this wonderful man I have met and am very happy with. Lovely children who I'm very proud of. I have so much to live for. I know the way I respond in emergency situations is to become quite calm.'

Although she was once a Christian and taught Bible class, God did not figure much in her thoughts while trapped. 'I have made bargains with God in the past and not kept them and I thought about that and I thought I'm not going there.'

Ann and Graham now intend to live life to the full, much as they did before the earthquake. '*Carpe diem* is our motto. Since 22 February we have lived each day with a renewed sense of happiness and gratitude for being alive. Life is good. Make the most of it,' says Ann.

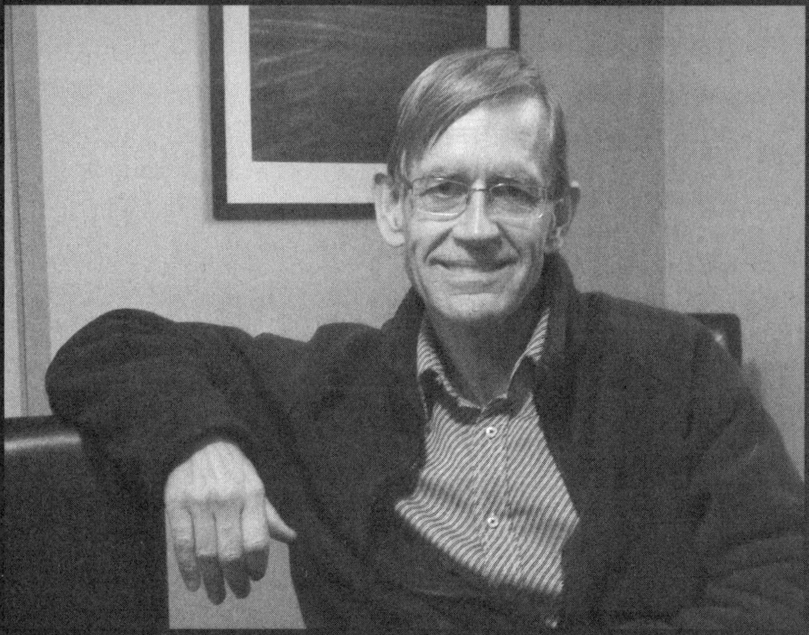

9

CHRIS LITTLEWOOD

'I thought at least we are alive and
we have a chance.'

A DEEP DARK HOLE in the place where he expected to see stairs is an image Chris Littlewood, 64, will never forget. Chris found himself looking into the abyss soon after the earthquake in Christchurch struck on 22 February. He was on the sixth floor of the landmark blue 17-storey Forsyth Barr building on the corner of Armagh and Colombo Streets.

'I remember the upward thrust because the other ones were more of a rattle. It was an incredible noise like the meshing of steel, almost like an explosion of rock,' says Chris, who as Assistant Ombudsman, runs the seven-staff Ombudsman's office in Christchurch. He dived under his desk and heard people screaming and crying.

'To this day I have no memory of how I found myself under the desk. Whether it was the upthrust of the earthquake which caused me to fall or whether it was something from childhood I don't know. I was brought up in Wellington and one of my first memories of going to school in Wellington was the fun we used to have during quake time when we had to scramble under the desks and then have an assembly out on the field.

'After the shaking I wandered out of the office and met up with the two women who are our admin secretaries and sort of in a dazed fashion went next door. I have been told I was white with shock and I was shivering with fear.

'I found myself standing beside one of the doors to the stairwell. I can remember looking at this tangle of reinforcing down into this cavernous gap. I can't have looked for long. It was enough to wonder how the dickens were we going to get out of this building. Here we were in one of the most modern buildings in town. We had comforted ourselves that if it withstood the September earthquake, it would withstand anything.'

'I loved that building,' says Chris, a former Dunedin lawyer and crown counsel. 'Each floor accommodated only about 20 people and just before the earthquake the owners had spent a lot of money refurbishing the foyer. I loved the view from my office. On a clear winter's day I could see the mountains.'

It weathered the September earthquake and subsequent aftershocks well, although he and his staff were worried about cracks in the stairwell landing, just outside the toilets. 'We were told the landing was OK and that the building behaved exactly the way it should. They said it was tied to the interior walls and although it has cracked a bit and might crack a bit more, nothing had affected its integrity. They were going to fill up the cracks with a bit of cement. That was the reassurance we lived with.'

Chris's office shared the sixth floor with law firm GCA Lawyers, which operates with 15 staff and specialises in class actions. After the terrifying shake, the floor's occupants gathered in the law office to consider their options. A GCA staff member had already written HELP on the window with a felt tip pen. They watched people streaming out of the nearby Copthorne Hotel and 20-storey PricewaterhouseCoopers building and cursed their own building, which felt like a prison, says Chris. Cellphone calls were not getting through and Chris was to learn afterwards that his wife Ruth, an Environment Canterbury planner who had been driving on Bealey Avenue, narrowly missed a deluge of bricks from the toppling Knox Church.

John Haynes, an investigator for the Ombudsman's Office, led the discussion in the boardroom, Chris remembers. 'He said we have an option. Either we could stay here and wait to be rescued or we could try to get out.'

Haynes is a recreational climber and has vast experience in search and rescue operations. He is also the author of several books, one on Tom Fyfe, the Timaru man who, with two others, was the first to climb Aoraki-Mt Cook, and another on New Zealand rugby league pioneers. He declined to be interviewed for this book but following the quake told reporters he was concerned at the time both about fire and the prospect of the building pancaking like the Twin Towers of the World Trade Center in New York on 11 September 2001. 'The guts of the building fell down seventeen storeys. We just had a shell of a building,' he later told *The Press* newspaper.

Chris, who had lost one of the lenses in his spectacles, says someone began to talk about ropes. His office had received several from its Wellington headquarters, well before the September earthquake, due to concerns raised by September 11. The ropes and a mallet were stored in a cabinet in the office. 'We looked at them when they arrived and I remember John saying, "These aren't much good. What on earth are we going to do with these?"'

But they were better than nothing and all the group had. 'I have this undying memory of John sitting on the floor and trying to work out what he was going to do with these ropes. He was working out how long they were and whether they were long enough to drop somebody out to the top of the carpark building about fifteen metres down.'

The rope was more than long enough and John was able to double it up for greater strength. Then came the question of who was first. John chose a young man of medium build from the lawyers' office, to test the ropes. Not everyone was keen to take the trip down to the carpark, although plenty of reassurance, says Chris, was coming from John and Grant Cameron, a former police officer and principal of GCA, who was helping John belay people to safety.

John Haynes, an investigator for the Ombudsman's Office, led the discussion in the boardroom, Chris remembers. 'He said we have an option. Either we could stay here and wait to be rescued or we could try to get out.'

'It was interesting to see the range of emotions,' says Chris. 'John was very cool and Grant was very much in charge. Clearly I was shocked and white with fear but I got through that. Then I thought, *The building has withstood that massive quake. The worst thing is that we could be here one or two days.* We did have a discussion about staying. Then we had another aftershock and the decision was sort of made for us.'

He sat with a woman, the mother of two school-age children, who was sobbing with fear. 'I tried to reassure her. She was one of the first to go. It was like the *Titanic*. I remember another woman whose body was pulsating with fear. She screamed when we got her to the window and put the rope over her head. She screamed "I can't go", and we had to put her back on the floor. She walked to one side sobbing with fear.

'In the end Grant and I actually lifted her over the ledge and down the side. And I can remember this scream. We said, "Keep those eyes closed until you get to the bottom."'

While they waited he and Grant's partner in the law firm, Maurice Walker, walked around the floor taking in the panoramic views of the city. 'We could see dust coming up from Colombo Street. We looked at the Cathedral and saw that the top had fallen and then saw a building which looked like a crushed set of cardboard boxes. It was the PGC building. The dust had gone and we wondered how many people could have survived that. Then we looked onto Colombo Street and saw the bricks and wondered how many people had been killed. It might have been this that shook me out of my shock. I thought at least we are alive and we have a chance.'

When it came to his turn for the descent, he grabbed his suit jacket because it contained his wallet. Grant was having none of that and took the jacket, tied the wallet into a sleeve with a knot and hurled it out the window. The descent held no fears for Chris. 'I trusted John absolutely. It was remarkably fortunate we had him.'

He then waited on the street to thank John. By this time, about 4 p.m., a crane from Christchurch firm Smith Crane and Construction was on the scene and John, Grant and others were brought down in a cradle. 'He got out in style. It was befitting,' Chris says.

Chris, a marathon runner, walked home and when he arrived, he received a call from his son Matthew, a reporter for the *Timaru Herald*, who interviewed him about the ordeal.

Looking back Chris says he will always admire John's coolness and says his experience has caused several small changes to his life. 'I feel a bit like those huntaway dogs. They're always on edge and have always got their noses in the air. You feel on edge and wonder what is going to happen next. You begin to think: you have worked all those years, sixty hours a week, isn't there more to life than that? It makes you hang on to good friends and we are in much closer contact with neighbours and people around us. I've always regarded myself as fortunate. That you should reflect on this and listen to the grieving of other people.'

He remains concerned evidence about the collapse of the stairs in the Forsyth Barr building and the damage to other buildings will be lost as demolition proceeds. 'If a fire had swept through that building soon after the earthquake – a real possibility – about 150 people could have been burnt to death.'

Helen Grice rehabilitating in Burwood Hospital, August 2011.

10

HELEN GRICE

'I thought I could go hysterical and start screaming and crying or calm myself down, focus on breathing, not go into shock and get through this.'

HELEN GRICE CALLS her earthquake accident a 'little domestic' disaster. While the 22 February earthquake in Christchurch took its toll mainly in the central city, the danger it posed for people still in their houses was also very real. In some suburbs rocks fell from the hills, shredding and crushing homes, but Helen, living on the flat, is one of the shake's severest suburban casualties with permanent paraplegia.

The mother of four – Matthew, 25, Simon, 20, Charlotte, 17, Henry, 15 – and wife of Ben, a computer engineer, was in the living room of her 80-year-old, two-storey home in Clyde Road, Fendalton, when the earthquake hit. She had her son Henry and nephew Rupert Scobie home from Christchurch Boys' High as the school was closed due to a teachers' stop-work meeting. Helen was standing in her family room, looking outside at a climbing rose, thinking it was about time to get those 'little brats' working instead of hooking up the Xbox. The family room had a flat roof and was below the second storey of the house, from which two chimneys protruded. One went through the peak of the roof and the other stood two metres above the roof line. Both chimneys had been damaged in the September quake and further weakened by tremors on Boxing Day but had stayed up.

Roofing contractors sent by the Earthquake Commission had inspected the chimneys only a week before the 22 February earthquake and judged them dangerous and needing to come down. Neither Helen nor Ben thought it was urgent. 'We thought the earthquakes were getting less frequent and thought, *We are in the system and they know what's going on*. We expected the eastern suburbs to get priority because they were a lot worse,' says Helen. She was going to give EQC a 'rark up' the next day if she hadn't heard anything by then.

When the house started to shake at 12.51 p.m. her first thought was this quake was different. 'It was sharper and had a mean bounce to it. I suddenly thought, *Oh shit, the chimney*, and tried to move away.'

She remembers hearing the chimney slide down the roof and having a distinct feeling of it coming to get her. 'I tried to run and the shaking pushed me and I fell further back. I was on the floor and clawing my way over the carpet and heard the roar. I thought, *Oh God, please let me live through this*. And then it hit me. I thought, *Oh, bloody hell. This is going to hurt*, and then the pain hit me.'

> 'I was on the floor and clawing my way over the carpet and heard the roar. I thought, *Oh God, please let me live through this*.'

The solid, two-metre high chimney, which stayed remarkably intact, had smashed through the living room roof iron and through 300 mm-by-125 mm exposed beams to hit Helen in the middle of her back. She had just managed to shove her head under a corner of her coffee table but the damage had been done. Helen was trapped under the chimney and in severe pain.

Her son Henry came running down the stairs but couldn't see his mother immediately, because she was hidden by the rubble. Helen, he would say later, looked like something out of a horror movie, as she was spitting blood from being hit in the mouth. While Rupert tried to lift debris off Helen, Henry waded across the Wairarapa Stream bordering the property to a building site to alert a group of builders, who rushed over to help.

Helen realised she had no control of her legs and was feeling something like an electrical current going up and down them. Her jaw and neck were also swelling dramatically from the blows to her head. Rupert, who had just finished an intensive first aid course, was worried about the builders moving her and Helen, 'because I'm the mother', had to enter the debate to explain it was more important to get her out. 'I thought I could go hysterical and start screaming and crying or calm myself down, focus on breathing, not go into shock and get through this. It was one of those life moments. My family were there and they were so stressed, I didn't want to add any more to the mix.'

The builders and the two boys tried to lift the chimney off Helen but it was too heavy, so one of the builders fetched a big crowbar and they managed to lever the chimney up high enough for Rupert to slide in and pull her out. The boys then got an ironing board to put against her back to stop any movement and wrapped her up in duvets and blankets.

One of the rescue crew was delivery driver Dave Chivell. 'All I saw were these amazingly tattooed legs,' Helen says. 'I said to him, "I know this sounds really ridiculous, but will you hold my hand?" I just wanted to connect back to humanity and I was really scared but did not want to show the boys.' Dave continued talking to Helen and holding her hand until the ambulance arrived three-and-a-half hours later.

With Helen lying on the floor in pain, the immediate concern was to get some medical help but the telephones were overloaded and not working. Henry and Rupert went out on the street to look for a doctor or nurse and neighbours were alerted. Eventually a neurosurgeon, who practises in Singapore, arrived on his bike. Helen could still feel her legs and feet being touched and this was a good sign, said the surgeon, who assured her she would survive.

In the end Helen was visited by a number of nurses and, she reckons, about four doctors. Her sister Liz Scobie (mother of Rupert), who was on duty at Christchurch Hospital where she works as a theatre nurse, was also on her way but was stuck in snarled up traffic. Meanwhile Helen had her team of core carers, Henry, Rupert and Dave, on the job. Henry reluctantly gave her some Panadol (without water because he was worried about internal injuries), which she chomped down 'like they were strawberries'. They also looked for cold compresses for the pain and cold towels were soon replaced by frozen peas. 'It was so calm, just like a bubble,' says Helen. 'People came in and out but we were a team.'

Finally her son Matthew rang from Auckland on the landline and coordinated an ambulance through the Auckland call centre. Ben, who was caught in traffic, was trying to get home from Sydenham and could not be contacted. He was not particularly worried about the earthquake, he says. 'It always happens to somebody else. I thought the chimney would come down but it wouldn't hurt anybody.'

But Helen was terrified, thinking that Ben might be injured as well. He arrived shortly before the ambulance, which drove in at 4.30 p.m., and watched as Helen was carefully put on a stretcher. By then her main thought was for morphine.

'I have been through childbirth without pain relief and this was worse. Towards the end I was thinking they have to get here soon because of the pain. I didn't know what had happened to my legs but I was sure they would fix that.'

In the ambulance the relief of morphine was elusive as the paramedics could not find a vein.

'I told them I wasn't paying their fifty-dollar fee because I was getting the budget ride,' Helen says.

At the hospital, the doors opened and it 'felt like the end of the Coast to Coast [a long distance race in the South Island]. It was like, *You've made it. Thank God, I've crossed the line. I'm battered and bruised but I'm here*. It was just the most warm feeling and then an aftershock came and the lights went out.'

She remembers snippets. Her daughter crying and a priest anointing her but not much else, other than confused and bizarre dreams.

She finally got her painkiller and a portable X-ray machine was brought over to take X-rays of her back. A doctor reached under her back, found something squishy and immediately suspected the worst. 'Then he said, "It's a bloody packet of peas." I said, "You'd better save those. They're for tonight's tea."

Helen had time to have a chat with the hospital chaplain, Sister Mary Hanrahan, her old headmistress at Villa Maria College, before going to the orthopaedic ward where, that night, she went downhill fast.

After an operation on Thursday night to stabilise her spine, Helen was put in the intensive care unit (ICU) and remained mainly unconscious, in an induced coma, for the next eight to 10 days. She remembers snippets. Her daughter crying and a priest anointing her but not much else, other than confused and bizarre dreams. 'It was like I was at the bottom of a swimming pool and trying to swim back to the surface and my hearing was very acute. I thought, *I'm glad we're not a society that puts people like me on an ice floe.* I felt so vulnerable and thought, *What if Christchurch is not there any more?*'

The heavy medication made her delusional and she thought Ben was playing a cruel joke by making her legs lifeless, and at one point she wondered how he had convinced John Key and Bob Parker to pretend there was an earthquake. On her first night out of ICU, she kept on hearing voices and Ben stayed with her all night.

Before she went to Burwood Hospital, medical staff were non-committal about whether she would walk again. 'Not knowing anything at all about what was happening started to become almost frightening.'

She learned that the spinal cord was not like the tough fibre-optic cable she had imagined it as. Instead it is more like toothpaste and most spinal injuries are caused by the vertebrae bruising or squashing it. 'I could still feel people touching my big toe and I had seen the movies where that meant you were OK and thought that was going to be me.'

Burwood Hospital was like entering a warm bubble.

'It was so positive and so supportive. I did not have the time to do the "what ifs". The nurses were just so amazing. When you are that desperate and that vulnerable you need people who think the way they do. I thought, *I'm not a vegetable. I'm a person. I have some benefit.* It stopped me having thoughts of depression. I can't say enough about the care and expertise of the staff at Burwood, and especially knowing they were in just as bad a state as my family. I had so much care and support, I felt obliged to recover.'

Her running joke was that Burwood Hospital was really the Burwood Day Spa and she would talk about facials and colonics and monogrammed dressing gowns.

Helen makes the adjustment process seem surprisingly straightforward although admits to having moments of despair. 'There are days when you want to scream. The first time I saw ladies' shoes on sale anywhere, I was just devastated. Somebody is off for a holiday somewhere and I think, *Oh bugger, I'll never leave a footprint on the beach.* The first time I saw myself in a wheelchair, I cried. I thought I would be, *Yay, I'm off the bed and going to get out and be independent.* I went past a mirror and just sobbed because it was the biggest shock I have had in my life. What happened to the Elle McPherson body and the six-foot legs? There was this short, dumpy, middle-aged lady trying to wheel herself around a room.'

With her children nearly off her hands, she had been wondering what to do with the rest of her life. 'I was lying there and thinking this is a life experience I didn't think I was ever going to have. I thought, you have a choice. You can go under or, scared as you are, you can just embrace everything they are telling you and learn as much as you can. And now, very dramatically, I have had my midlife crisis and I am learning new things and new experiences and I have somehow managed to make myself comfortable with it. I don't see it as life is over. If this had happened to me in my early twenties or thirties, it would have been devastating. I'm lucky I've lived a full life and have had choices that haven't been dictated by mobility. Now I feel that I'm comfortable. I'm not looking back and thinking, *I used to be able to do this and that.* Although it's true that I still have my moments when I have a good sob in the shower because I think this is so enormous.

'Most of the time, I think if I can learn to use the skills they are teaching me, I can have independence. The biggest thing I was frightened about was that I would be left sitting at home like a video on pause waiting for the family to show up so life could start for me that day. I want to be able to get in the car because I'm really looking forward to those mobility parking spaces and as long as I can carry on and do those normal things, it's bearable.'

At first she felt as though her body was split in half and the bits that could not move did not belong to her. One day in the shower she looked down at her feet and thought, *You poor things*, and from there the reunion started.

One of the hardest things to cope with is the change in the centre of gravity, she says. 'They teach you skills like getting from wheelchair to the bed. I couldn't even remember how to sit up. They teach you how to manoeuvre yourself without help. I now balance myself from just under my bra line and that is incredibly wobbly. You feel you are constantly sitting on a board balancing on a Swiss Ball, so you are always wobbling.'

Having two other women with very similar earthquake injuries in Burwood – Marie Mackey (Chapter 12) and Beverley Edwards – helped enormously, Helen says.

'You've got somebody to talk to about how you are going to live through this process. How desirable are you going to be? We are all talking about this. How does a husband go from seeing you at death's door to somebody who is a sexual being. Physically, you can't wee and poo by yourself any more. You have to learn these things to survive. All of us are coming to points that we can't get our heads around and to be able to talk amongst ourselves about it is a big thing.'

She shares a room with Marie Mackey and says they pull each other through the bad times. 'One is down when the other is up.'

The future looks slightly intimidating, Helen says. She expects to come home for good at the end of the August but wonders what sort of home, as the Clyde Road house is currently undergoing major repairs and the family are in rental accommodation.

'I'm just getting over the shock and awe of being out in the public. I'm only going to be three foot tall for the rest of my life. I'll always be staring at people's navels. The first time I stay home by myself and the first time I go to the shops by myself. Those things loom very large at the moment.

'I haven't been given a death sentence. My life was this box over here and somehow I have been plucked out and put in another box, but I still have the way I want to live my life. I still want to make a nuisance of myself at my son's wedding or be there for my daughter's graduation. There are still things I want to do whether I am in a wheelchair or not. I'll just get better parking and I'll get to sit up front.

'The danger is you can keep mourning for what you have lost and forget there is living going on around you at the moment. What went through my mind as I was under the chimney and waiting for the ambulance was that I want to be part of this family. I don't want to let go of it.

'And whatever way, shape or form it comes, I will take it, because it's life. So even way back at the beginning I knew it was going to be a challenge but I didn't want to lose that challenge. I felt euphoric when I was coming out of everything because I had survived. It feels a bit churlish to come out the other end to say, "I have got this package now and I'm not that happy with it."

'I've had so much reassurance from within my family that I'm still important. I got to the right people at the right time for my recovery and still have my family around me.'

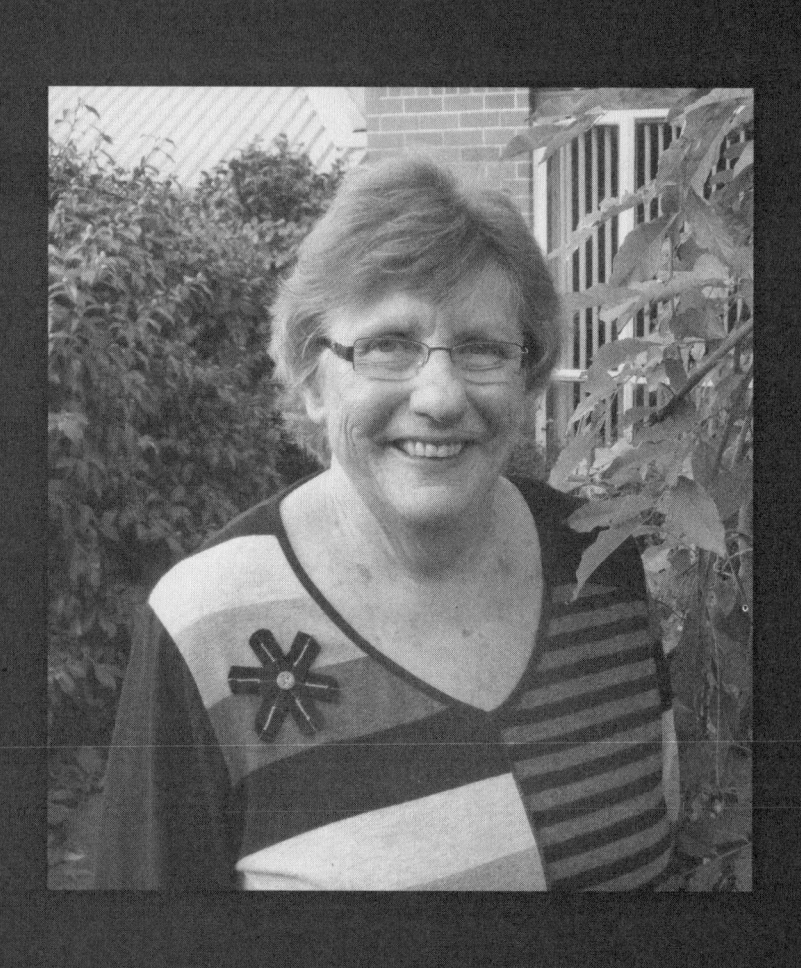

11

ANNE MALCOLM

'The next bit I remember is being under jagged rubble and being compressed by broken stuff and it being quite dark.'

NOT LONG AFTER riding five levels down in an imploding building, a still conscious Anne Malcolm found herself sitting on stony ground nearby. Still stunned, she was not sure of what had happened and was unaware she had been pulled from the rubble by police and then carried to the bare ground. Barry Grottis, a student from the New Zealand Institute of Sport, had stopped, bandaged her badly broken arm and given her water. Anne told Barry her name. She was wearing a brown T-shirt, loose-fitting jeans and sandals. Dried blood covered one side of her face and despite her recent ordeal she was still wearing her glasses.

All this is known not from Anne but mostly from a now famous photograph taken as she was sitting on stones with the collapsed Canterbury Television (CTV) building in Madras Street behind her. The photograph, taken by a *Christchurch Star* photographer and used around the world, conveyed much about the Christchurch earthquake of 22 February. It could not, however, relay the extent of her severe injuries. She had a gash to her head, a broken pelvis, complicated breaks in her ribs, a broken thigh bone, a shoulder that had been ripped out of its socket and an arm in which the tendons had been cut.

The former dietitian could have retired years ago from her position at the counselling agency Relationship Services, which occupied the fifth level of the building. The organisation grew out of Marriage Guidance and now does a wide variety of counselling, including work with trauma patients. After her marriage broke up, Anne took her four girls to Christchurch where they all went to university. She became clinical leader of the service and retired in 2006 only to return part-time to the 'shop floor' to work as a counsellor.

Anne wasn't rostered to work on the Tuesday of the earthquake but had gone in for a cultural supervison meeting with Louise Tankersley, the service's cultural advisor. 'I was going on holiday with the family for a week and I thought I would go in for the 12 o'clock meeting and see a couple of clients in the afternoon and clean up some paperwork.'

> 'The counsellors on the opposite side of the window seemed to surf down on one of the walls. The roof came down and there were four or five of the counsellors who were actually fully conscious through the whole thing . . .'

The meeting was normally held in a windowless room in the centre of the floor. When Anne walked in at 11.50 a.m., one of the other counsellors suggested moving to a family room on the outside corner of the building with windows on two sides. Ten counsellors, including two male counsellors, were at the meeting, and Louise also brought her eight-month-old baby. 'He is a very happy baby. He just gets passed around and gets cooed at and enjoyed and sits on the floor and takes notice of everybody,' Anne says.

Clinical leader Pablo Godoy was next door doing some paperwork and administrator Nina Bishop, who was killed in the collapse, was at her desk.

'We were all sitting in a circle on chairs. My memory is bit intermittent but what I recall is an absolute explosion in the room. So quickly did it happen, I don't recall thinking, *Earthquake*. It just impacted with explosive force and then the next bit I remember is being under jagged rubble and being compressed by broken stuff and it being quite dark and not really being able to work out what had happened.

'I did hear somebody call my name and I had heavy pressure on my chest. I remember summoning up enough breath to call out,

"I'm here." I remember saying that and really don't have an accurate memory beyond that moment until I was lying on the grass in Latimer Square.'

Anne has managed to piece together what happened from talking to the police officers who rescued her and the other counsellors in the room. All survived, although four had serious injuries. Louise and her baby escaped without major injury.

'The counsellors on the opposite side of the window seemed to surf down on one of the walls. The roof came down and there were four or five of the counsellors who were actually fully conscious through the whole thing and they were able to identify where we all were. When the dust settled, they have told me they didn't realise the building had come completely down because they were all so thrown around in the impact. They knew they were looking at rubble where we had been, so when the five police officers arrived on the scene, they were able to say there is somebody there and these young guys were able to rip into that rubble and found us, which is extraordinary because at that stage the aftershocks were continuing and also a fire had started at the service end of the building where the lifts were.'

She doesn't remember being attended to in the street but Barry told her afterwards that she had been conscious and given her name. She has no memory of being dragged from the rubble and was able to tell a police officer, who felt terrible about the pain he must have caused her, that she couldn't remember a thing.

She does remember the extraordinary organisation of the triage base in Latimer Square where she was looked after by two women paediatricians, who were in Christchurch for a conference. At the triage base Anne was also reunited with her handbag and her cellphone, which enabled her to get in touch with her daughters. 'It was pretty traumatic for Jen [in Auckland] who rang to find it answered by someone who, at that point, didn't know if I was alive. Eventually this counsellor saw me being carried over and put the phone to my ear, and I recall saying, "Yes. I'm absolutely fine."'

Jen, a lawyer, is one of Anne's four high-achieving daughters. Robyn is better known to New Zealanders as the actress who played the tough, fiery matriarch in the Westie drama *Outrageous Fortune*. Suze is a clinical psychologist and mother of two in Wellington and Jo, who has three children, is a former television journalist and now journalism tutor at the University of Canterbury. Jo is also married to Roger Sutton, who, as chief executive of the Canterbury Earthquake Recovery Authority, is in charge of the agency now leading the reconstruction of Christchurch.

In Latimer Square, people were screaming and the doctors pinned various notes to Anne's clothing. 'I never felt like I would not make it. I didn't feel extreme pain. I remember being in the ambulance and being reassured as we bumped and rolled around. And then I remember the hospital entry which looked like the set of *ER*, all business, and feeling this amazing reassurance at the competence of medical staff and I remember feeling safe.'

Almost immediately she was taken into theatre for an operation on her cut arm and tendons but it was not until three or four days later that the damage to her left shoulder and arm was discovered. Her arm was reattached in an operation performed by an Auckland orthopaedic team who had flown to Christchurch to help.

After Anne was taken to hospital by ambulance, and later put in a ward, her family temporarily lost contact with her. That first night no-one knew exactly where she was. The first person to see her the next morning was Roger Sutton, who managed to track her down with the help of someone in the hospital. She soon had the comfort of family visits and once staff knew about her famous daughter, a bit of vicarious celebrity. Anne was very worried about a patient who she knew had arrived for an appointment with her and who had been waiting in the waiting room. Nurses were able to tell her the young woman was two doors down and had a broken back.

Being a counsellor has helped her own recuperation, she says. 'I'm OK. I'm up and down a bit but I know what to expect and I know what trauma does to people and recognise symptoms in myself. There was a splendid young psychologist at Burwood [Hospital] and I said, "No, I'm fine," and she didn't give up and she just kept coming because there were times when I did want to talk to her about stuff. Stuff did appear out of left field. She was really good at helping me pre-empt what happened next. She said the transition from hospital to home would be really hard and it was.'

Anne returned home just before Easter. She does not have flashbacks or nightmares but does not sleep well and faces some tough times when she gets her mobility back. 'If I think about going into a high-rise building I think, *No*. If I think about a movie or lift, I think, *No, no, no*. I can't go anywhere at the moment, but I wonder which supermarket I will go to. The thought of small spaces or enclosed spaces brings up a bit of panic. Police reckon I was under a metre of rubble. I can't describe it but I can feel it.'

She often thinks about the young people killed in the collapse. 'We saw the kids up and down in the lifts all the time. The language school kids were coming and going and they would practise their language skills on us and they were enormously polite and respectful. We would pass the time of day and the door would open and we could see the language school.

'I can get really angry about that building. I want the inquiry to be really comprehensive. If there is an answer to that building going down I want that answer found. I don't know what I will do. I've got questions I want answered. Was there a fundamental flaw in that building? I want to know that. I hope there wasn't. I hope there will be no glossing over and I don't think there will be.'

Relationship Services had been in the building well over 10 years and at one point shared the fifth floor with a fitness training company. After Christchurch's September earthquake, some who worked in the building felt it was unsafe but Anne was not one of them.

'After September I was confident the building was a safe structure. We were told the reason it rolled in the earthquake was because it was constructed on rubber roller foundations and this meant it was extraordinarily safe. It felt frightening in aftershocks. We were all in a meeting on October 20 [2010] and we rolled around and were all shaken up. The building rolled and we rolled with it and we didn't vacate the floor. The young people in the language school rushed outside and Civil Defence told us we had done the right thing by staying exactly where we were.'

In the last months of 2010 the building next door was demolished because of damage sustained in the September earthquake. The demolition sometimes felt like an earthquake and by December, says Anne, everyone was getting pretty agitated. 'We were just fed up with the noise of the demolition and the impact it had on our building. Some counsellors thought [our building] was dodgy but I personally did not because I trusted it had been inspected by the people who I believed knew what they were doing. The word had come through that the building had stood up and performed exactly how it was supposed to.'

Anne had believed the building had the same sort of foundation as that used in the construction of the national museum, Te Papa Tongarewa, in Wellington. Te Papa is supported by an earthquake absorption technology called Lead Rubber Bearings, which was developed by the University of Canterbury engineer Dr Bill Robinson. The technology is now sold by Wellington company Robinson Seismic Ltd, which says the technology was not used in the CTV building and no staff member ever visited it.

'This belief gave me extraordinary faith in the building,' says Anne. 'After September 4, when clients were coming for earthquake support counselling, and had difficulty accepting we were on the fifth floor and were pretty frightened, the first thing I would say was, "This is one of the safest buildings in Christchurch.' I told them if there was an aftershock the building would roll like we are on a jelly but that was part of its safety. I said to many clients, "If this building has come down, the whole of Christchurch has come down." That was the degree of confidence I had in that building.'

There is no escaping the fact the once active, fit, energetic Anne, who has never really been sick, has experienced a radical change in her normal life. She gets grumpy at times and has to remind herself what she went through. Her days are busy with physiotherapy.

> 'Initially I was euphoric. I survived, I survived. Now I'm up and down. Some days I feel despondent but my friends are the same. Life has changed fundamentally.'

'I'm completely dependent and there is a lot I can't do. I'm not as positive as I was. I always had heaps of energy and now that runs dry. Initially I was euphoric. I survived, I survived. Now I'm up and down. Some days I feel despondent but my friends are the same. Life has changed fundamentally. When I feel grumpy, I say to myself, "Hang on a minute. You have to be grateful." I am, but I sometimes kick against that.

'I wish I hadn't been in the building and wish I hadn't gone to that meeting that day. So I vacillate between being grateful and being resentful it even happened. In the long-term rehabilitation I am really sticking to one day at a time.'

She can't see herself getting back to work as a counsellor any time soon. 'Not in the immediate future. Even if could physically cope, I am really clear I couldn't be with people and be alongside them with their problems and chaos. I haven't got that in me.'

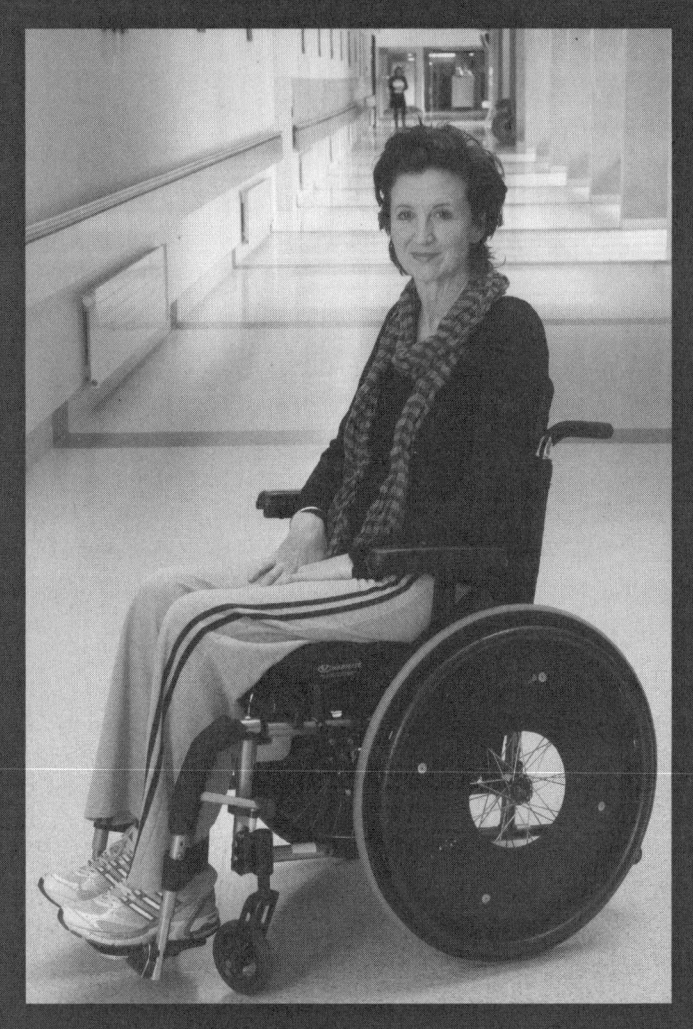

Marie Mackey in Burwood Hospital, August 2011.

12

MARIE MACKEY

'The world stopped. Life stopped.'

MARIE MACKEY JUST catches herself before she says, 'I'll see you to the door.' Left a paraplegic by the 22 February earthquake in Christchurch, such small, automatic gestures are presently beyond her but sometimes she still reacts as though she has use of her legs.

Marie, a patient of the Burwood Hospital Spinal Unit since March, is home for a precious afternoon and evening. Her recovery from multiple injuries has been slow and hard and her goal of getting back to work as a client director for Gen-i, part of the Telecom group that provides technology systems to a wide range of public and private organisations, seems a long way off.

On a Sunday afternoon in late June, with much of winter still ahead, many things are still uncertain. The home she shares with daughter Kate, 13, and husband Petter Evans, a wine maker and viticulturist for Sherwood Estate in Waipara, was badly damaged in the earthquakes of 4 September 2010 and 22 February 2011 and Petter is packing up the house they have lived in for 11 years in readiness for the builders. In addition to getting the house cleared, Petter will have to co-ordinate urgently needed repairs and the added complication of getting the house ready for wheelchair access. What should be a straightforward exercise has the potential to turn into a nightmare as architects, builders, the Earthquake Commission, ACC and insurance companies try to work together. Marie could be ready to leave Burwood by September but doesn't know yet if she will be going to a rest-home, a motel, a rented house or back to her remodelled home.

In what now can only be seen as an irony, when the earthquake hit, she had just picked up a pair of shoes from the well-known Bennetts shoe repair shop in Colombo Street. The shoes were a pair of Marie's

> Only Marie's head and part of her arm were visible in the rubble and he thought she was dead. He lifted her head slightly and when she groaned realised she was still alive.

favourite work shoes and Bennetts had redone the heels. 'I was keen to get them back because each morning I would go into the wardrobe and think, *I can't wear those*. I needed that height of shoe. I don't know why I just didn't buy a new pair.'

Her EFTPOS transactions show she paid at exactly 12.50 p.m. 'In the next sixty seconds, the world stopped. Life stopped.'

She has no memory of what happened and did not emerge from an induced coma for 10 days. Photographs of where she was found show large sections of concrete and piles of bricks lying on Colombo Street outside Bennetts and the High Country Outdoors recreation shop next door. The upper-storey façade of the High Country Outdoors shop is on the ground and the tents on the upper floor can be seen like furniture in a doll's house.

Buried under rubble, Marie was spotted by Cam Stewart, an experienced ski patroller, who was the manager of the Macpac shop further up Colombo Street. After the tremors stopped and the dust cleared he had gone looking for survivors. Only Marie's head and part of her arm were visible in the rubble and he thought she was dead. He lifted her head slightly and when she groaned realised she was still alive. He took charge, telling some bystanders to leave and others to start digging a path to her. She was lying in water, and the pungent smell of gas was in the air, clearly coming from a broken pipe somewhere nearby.

After about 10 minutes of digging and removing rubble, Cam and his crew lifted Marie onto a flat camping mattress and wrapped her in a sleeping bag. He checked her over and knew she needed to get to hospital quickly. Three ambulance crews on their way to other places in the central city declined to take her, although one gave Cam a neck brace. Eventually she was lifted into a police car and Cam jumped in to help take her to the hospital.

On the way they went past a chaotic scene on the corner of Lichfield and Manchester Streets, where other people were trapped, and an emergency specialist checked Marie and reinforced the urgency of getting her to hospital. About an hour after being pummelled by rubble, Marie was finally getting the specialist care she desperately needed. But she was far from well. A haematoma on her head was putting pressure on her brain and the severity of the impact to her head is thought to have caused the two breaks that were found in her spine. She also had a broken sternum and ribs. Her pelvis was fractured in five places, her ankle was broken and she had internal injuries. Her entire body was covered in angry bruises.

Marie was stabilised by emergency doctors and taken to the orthopaedic ward but within hours had to be resuscitated as her condition deteriorated rapidly. Because the lifts in the hospital were not working, she had to be carried down two flights of stairs in a bean bag to the Intensive Care Unit (ICU).

Petter was at work in Waipara and felt little of the earthquake. A text message from Kate alerted him to the severity of the shake and he drove in and picked her up from school. He tried to get hold of Marie but the phones were overloaded and he thought she would soon come walking through the door. But by 5 p.m. he was getting desperate and jumped on his bike. He cycled through Hagley Park and at a cordon was directed to Latimer Square. Meanwhile a nurse in Christchurch Hospital had recognised Marie and called Marie's manager at Gen-i, who contacted Petter. 'To hear Marie was in ICU I was absolutely beside myself,' Petter says.

They spent the next 10 days in hospital as Marie fought for her life. She had an operation to stabilise her spine and release pressure on her brain and eventually her condition improved. She was then sent back to the orthopaedic ward, where she slowly came out of her induced coma. 'When I woke up fully I remember thinking, *I will just walk out of here*. When I was told I had paraplegia, apparently I said, "I don't need any of that. You can take it away,"' Marie says.

Marie had lost her short term memory temporarily and had to be reminded she couldn't walk. 'We didn't know how severe the brain injury was. It was certainly clear she had a severe injury and slowly, in bits and pieces, we got more information. To know she was mentally there was such a relief,' Petter says.

After two weeks in Christchurch Hospital, Marie was transferred to Burwood Hospital. There it was discovered she had 700 ml of fluid – enough for a wine bottle, says Petter – on her lung and she needed another procedure to remove it. She was also unable to get into a wheelchair for several weeks and when rehabilitation started she had to wear a brace.

The severity of Marie's injuries means every step forward is often compromised. 'It's been one thing after another,' says Petter.

Once she arrived in Burwood, the fact she was a paraplegic – she has normal movement in her arms and hands but no feeling or control below her lower chest – began to sink in. 'It was a long time before I was comfortable in a wheelchair. Just to find you can't do the most basic movements is really hard. It's very hard work.'

When Marie was 13, her mother died in Burwood Hospital from cancer and Marie says it felt very weird to find herself in Burwood with a 13-year-old daughter, who must be feeling a lot like she did all those years ago.

Independent from an early age, Marie is used to being in control, a great contrast to her new life in which she is having to learn independence all over again. Seemingly small things add up. 'I've got a cupboard full of shoes that are no good to me any more. You have to buy bigger shoes because your feet swell. It just goes on the list of things. I suddenly find myself in runners which I can't even run in and track pants because I can't have seams in my clothing. My whole life I have been in control of everything, and this is just unbelievably different.'

Marie is not sure she has come to terms with how her life has changed. She still gets angry when she thinks how the old shop façades were so obviously dangerous and nothing was done. 'It just feels like on 22 February my whole life came to a stop. Everything that we had planned to do came to big stop. Then you are slowly picking up the pieces and it's a totally different direction. We used to travel a bit and had planned a trip to Europe this year. I can't even begin to think about travelling at the moment.

'I seem to manage to get through. Various people have suggested antidepressants but I don't want to numb myself out of this. At times I feel desperately unhappy but I don't want to make it all smooth as some of these drugs might do for you. I would rather have the feelings.

'I go between being resilient and not being resilient. You fluctuate, depending on how you are feeling. I know what I want to do and I would just like to get on and do it and sometimes it's just overwhelming. Just getting dressed can still be exhausting. It can all be totally frustrating. You just realise there is so much to learn and it just drives me nuts. Why do I have to do this? What did I do?'

Going back to work is one of Marie's main goals and she misses the stimulation of the job and her workmates. But there are some mountains to be climbed first. 'I want to go back to work and so I start to see these small glimpses of how hard life is going to be. I thought, *Oh good. I will be able to drive*, and that's the intention but you suddenly realise how physical it is to get in and out of a car. You are trying to fight this body that won't do what you are trying to make it do. And these big gaps open up and I think, *How am I going to get there?* I realise how tiring it is going to be and that is what I need to concentrate on in the next six months. I need to concentrate on that stamina.'

> 'It just feels like on 22 February my whole life came to a stop. Everything that we had planned to do came to big stop.'

Survivors of near-death experiences often profess to a new appreciation of life but Marie, who has almost constant nausea, says she doesn't sit around thinking how wonderful it is, although she does value family and friends more. 'Overall I'm glad I'm alive and being with my family is a very important part of that and then there are dark moments when you feel really stark. I do feel fortunate to be alive but it mainly relates to my family.'

Petter, who was into his busiest time in the vineyard three weeks after the accident, is clearly a rock for Marie and adds they have seen Marie steadily improve. 'It has not been a straight line. It's been up and down and to know she has been getting better is just the best thing. It's underestimated, what Marie has been through. Just to get from Colombo Street to the hospital was such a major thing. There is such a strong will to live that I'm confident she will use that to drive her to do the rest of the things. And I am confident as I can be that she will get back to work and the independence she requires.

'I don't know how you could do that to somebody's body and still have them come through. A head injury like Marie's can take twelve months to come right, so her frequent nausea is not uncommon. We see people dealing with wheelchairs and doing quite well and hope we can do that too.

'I feel she is getting stronger. A lot of it is just having the confidence to say you can do it. I remind Marie of what it would be like if she was not here. The loss of seeing Kate growing up, for instance. I think all families in situations like this grasp on to whatever they can. We are just so lucky to have Marie and we try to remind her as much as we can and give her as much love and support as we can.'

Marie says it's fantastic to have Helen Grice (Chapter 10), another paraplegic who was injured in the earthquake, in her room. 'For Helen and me, I hope we go out about the same time because we would be quite lost without each other.'

Experiencing the two earthquakes on 13 June in Christchurch as a paraplegic was frightening, says Marie. 'I can't move. I'm in a wheelchair, so where do I go to make myself safe? That Monday our door came off its runners and the nurses got all of us outside.'

Marie still asks 'Why me?' It is not as though she was taking risks or in a dangerous pursuit or occupation. Petter's view is that the accident shows the utter randomness of life. 'There is no rhyme or reason for it. She wasn't even driving a car. It just reflects the vulnerability of life.'

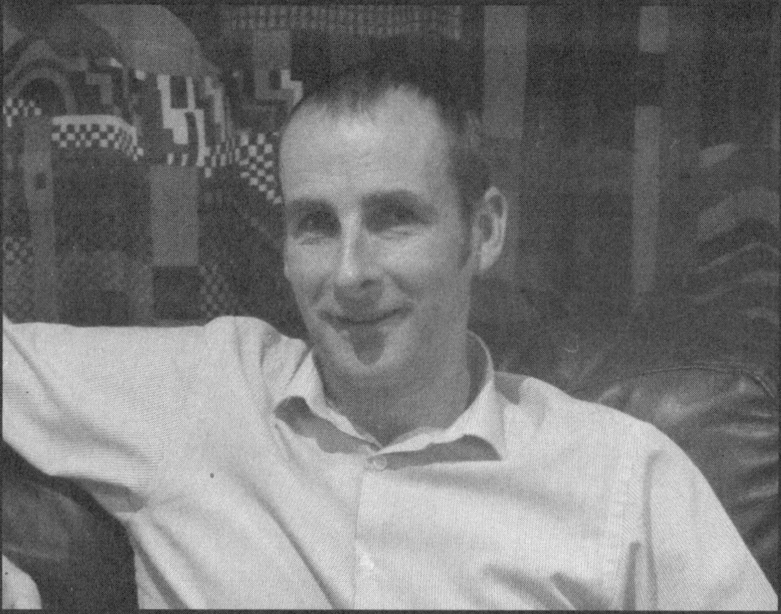

13

JIM FAITHFULL

'It had crossed my mind that this is it.
But I was thinking, *I'm still here. It's all right.*'

JIM FAITHFULL STRETCHED out in the total blackness of his tiny vault. That helped the agony in his back and as the pain mercifully subsided he tried to make himself comfortable and felt some hope returning.

That morning Jim, an Englishman from Essex, who had met his New Zealand wife Jacqui on her OE in England, had packed his lunch – a muffin, two muesli bars, ham and mustard sandwiches, and a peach – and gone to work as normal in the Pyne Gould Corporation (PGC) building in Cambridge Terrace. He had worked there for four years as an administration officer for Perpetual, a division of Pyne Gould that deals with estates, trusts and investment management. He was at his desk beside the windows on the east side of the building when it shuddered in a violent tremor.

After the September earthquake the previous year, he had wondered how the building would stand up to the 'big one' but the consensus was the building was solid and secure. 'It started off as pretty much all the other aftershocks did. A bit of a rumble and then it progressed to something bigger and bigger. I had time to sit there and to think, *This is getting quite big*, for probably three for four seconds. It was much bigger than I wanted it to be and I just got under my desk.'

Jim is not a huge man but the space available under the desk was such that his head was forced against his knees and his back pressed hard up against the desk top. 'I was conscious of a lot of movement, noise and wind. And then it all went pitch-black. I was initially stuck in a turtle position but once I had managed to pop myself out of that, because it was agony, I was able to straighten up. I knew I was in pain but thought I was all right.'

As it turned out later, being squashed under the desk fractured two vertebrae in his spine. He also cracked a rib, cut his head and received a number of bruises and cuts. 'It was very difficult to work out what had happened because it was pitch-black. I thought I had aggravated my back, which is not great anyway. As time went on I realised I had done something to it.

'I managed to pop my legs sideways and get over on my right hip. My legs had straightened out and I got into the recovery position. I had about 45 degrees' movement which meant I could roll from being right over on my side to sort of straightening out on my buttocks and my back.

'It remained completely dark. I didn't panic but it was really difficult because you can't work out which way is what and if you were going to go somewhere, where to go? It's frustrating. I'm quite a visual person so it was very difficult. Mind you, it was probably a good thing because I have no visual memories of what it was like in there.

'It had crossed my mind that this is it. But I was thinking, *I'm still here. It's all right.* The aftershocks kept going which was pretty terrifying but luckily for us they did not cause any more movement of the building. Things wobbled but nothing major.

'Pretty quickly after the shake, I started taking stock. I was feeling around looking for ways to get out but couldn't see anything. I could just make out my watch, which was giving out a slight light but that was the only thing I could see. I quickly established I could not get out of there.'

Jim knew he had concrete about a foot above his head by feeling around. When he had cleared the glass and rubble from beneath him to create a space to lie in, he started calling for help as loudly as he could. Some survivors in the building were able to communicate with the outside with their cellphones, but Jim's had been on his desk and was flat anyway.

His shouts for help went unheeded and to conserve his voice he called out less frequently. It was on one of those occasions, with his voice almost gone, that he finally made contact about 1 a.m., almost 12 hours after the quake. 'It was quite odd. I could hear quite a lot of what was going on outside but they couldn't hear me. I was yelling my head off. I was tapping on the concrete and pipes with a spoon I had in my desk and doing SOS and that sort of stuff. I could hear people chatting about what they were doing and cheers when people got out. A crane went past me. I could hear the hydraulics. A few noises also came from within the building.

'Some of it sounded close but mostly the drilling and stuff was distant. I could hear the fire brigade talking outside but not in loud voices. I couldn't work out why they couldn't get hold of me because I was shouting my head off. It took twelve hours before anybody heard me outside.'

One small mercy was that he was not alone. Although they could hear each other only if they shouted, he and fellow worker Helen Guiney were in constant contact. 'Once I got myself out of the agony, I could hear her cries for help. She was less than two metres away. I could hear other voices at various times. Some voices sounded painful and some were cries for help. Helen was a regular under her desk in the aftershocks. If there was a decent aftershock she didn't like them and had suffered some damage at her home. I made sure we were keeping in contact. I had no idea how bad her hand was. Having someone to talk to was helping me deal with it all as well. If I had been alone it would have been horrendous. Alone, in a pitch-black place.'

Helen, who had two injured and painful fingers – she would lose the tip of one – and who was also in total blackout, said afterwards it was the contact with Jim that kept her going. 'I don't know if I would have remained as calm if I were completely alone. I think I would have gone off the deep end.'

Another colleague, receptionist Ann Vos, could also hear Jim, although he could not hear her. But the fact that he was audible to her proved to be crucial for Jim's wife Jacqui. Jacqui, who worked in credit control for the plumbing and drainlaying firm Divers, was having 'a day out on the job with the boys' in Dallington when the quake hit. Jacqui watched the drainage trucks almost tip over as the ground spewed up sand and water from the pressure of liquefaction. It took two hours for her to get home in a trip that would normally take 15 minutes. She left messages on Jim's phone saying, 'I don't know where you are but if you get this can you go and get the kids?'

Later when she went to Christchurch Hospital to report Jim missing she caught the six o'clock news which had coverage of the phone call Ann made from the building to her son in Australia. In the phone call, to Jacqui's great relief, Ann mentioned that Jim was all right.

In the meantime, Jim had started on his lunch. He saved the peach because he thought he might need it later when he was thirsty. He never got around to eating it. By holding the watch a certain way he could just make out its luminous hands and could work out what the time was. 'The time went very slowly. It seemed to last for a hell of a long time. Looking back it was over in a flash but at the time it was different. Helen and I dozed off a couple of times but always woke up quickly because we had to make contact.'

He and Helen would shout to each other as soon as a lull in the drilling and banging occurred. They could hear Helen's cellphone ringing but Helen could not reach it.

'It was very frustrating because there were a number of conversations I started up with people on the outside and I thought they were responding to me but they were talking to someone else. That happened loads. I didn't know where the voices were coming from. I thought they were coming from the east side. I was concerned they might go away. Not knowing what was going on, I was thinking, *This is huge, and this is not exactly a massive building. How long are they going to be here before they go off to somewhere where there are more people?* That was a constant worry.'

Another worry was the rescuers might inadvertently kill him. 'I worried that rescuers might dislodge something. There was some quite heavy sounding machinery and it was cutting through the floors. Some sounded too heavy-duty to be going on above me. It sounded like any minute it was going to come through. It was a big steel thing that any minute was going to come down into my shoulder.'

He did not worry unduly about his family. He knew Jacqui was out on the road and that their children Ollie, 5, and Isobel, 7, were at school and in all likelihood safe.

Like many of those trapped, Jim could not avoid sooner or later having to relieve himself, although he held on for as long as he could. 'I was bursting. Sometime in the evening the pain of my bladder was nearing the pain in my back, so I had to do something about it. I got it as far as away as possible. Luckily I had a bottle of aftershave in my drawer and I got some paper out of my drawer and put that down. With the aftershave, it smelt quite pleasant in there.'

The hoped-for contact with rescuers about 1 a.m. did not mean instant release. 'They said they were on the way and were doing what they could to get to us out and were cutting through floors to get down to us. They said to hang in there, that this would take some time. They were shouting and they strained to hear me.'

Eventually rubble was cleared and Jim saw torchlight, 'a little spot of light' shining through a gap. 'It was pretty good to see that first torch beam. Sometimes they needed to swap with someone else and they would say, "I'll be back in a few minutes." I said, "Please don't go." They left the torch there. They took debris away and had to saw through some steel from the suspended ceiling to get to me.

'Eventually they made a tunnel to me and pulled me out by the hands. They got me to the bottom of the shaft and I was still on my stomach at this point. A fireman called Pete was the one pulling me out. I spent ten minutes holding his hands and looking into his eyes. When I got under the beam I had to turn over and do a ninety degree bend and then I passed out from the pain. They managed to get a harness on and winched me up to the top.

'As I was at the bottom of the shaft, there were quite a few heads on the way up and several heads peering over the top and it was lovely to see their faces. I don't remember if there was clapping. There could have been. I didn't look back. I was just elated to be out.'

When Jim was brought out on a stretcher about 9.40 a.m., Helen Guiney was already out, making him the next-to-last person to come out of the building alive. The last was Ann Bodkin (Chapter 8), who recalled hearing someone calling out from below her during the night. It was probably Jim.

Jacqui had been notified and made her way to the site. Jim, who is not given to extravagant emotion, says, 'It was very nice to see her. I was so relieved and making jokes with the rescuers. Life felt pretty good at that stage.'

Jim was in hospital for two or three days and heard about his colleagues over the next day or so. 'Work people came in to see me and I got word of who had survived and who had not. It did not surprise me so many died. I was surprised it was not more. Anybody who came out of that building had won the lottery.'

His workmate Brian Coker, an investment adviser, did not quite win the lottery but did survive in remarkable circumstances. Brian, 52, was walking down the stairs when the earthquake hit and was crushed by a falling concrete wall which landed on his legs. Thinking he was going to die, he sent a text telling his wife he loved her and might not survive. Rescuers arrived about 7 p.m. and Christchurch Hospital anaesthetist Bryce Curran and Australian urological surgeon Lydia Johns Putra used a hacksaw and a Leatherman fold-out knife to amputate both his legs. Brian, whose fight-back ability is now legendary, was back at work within six months.

By July, Jim's back is much improved. He credits his laidback and straightforward nature with helping him get over the ordeal, although he slept with the night-light on for three months.

The family also had to deal with another earthquake-related tragedy. Jacqui's uncle and aunt, Earl and Beverley Stick, were killed when their bus was crushed by falling debris in Colombo Street. Jim's sister and father came to Christchurch for a spell to help and his sister went to the funerals with him. By the time they left Jim was ready to return to work on a part-time basis. The company's 50 staff had occupied the whole first floor of the PGC building and 29 were in the building when it crumpled on 22 February. Of the 18 killed in the building, 10 were Perpetual employees, and Jim says that in the aftermath of the tragedy, he and his workmates are much closer.

'In the office there is good sense of camaraderie and being part of a family. It feels like an extended family. We've talked through our dark times. Everyone who could make it was at the funerals. We're all very, very thankful we are still here and really sorry we have lost our colleagues but there is also an element of getting on with it.'

Jim wonders if he would work in a multi-storey building again and admits the experience has prompted him and Jacqui to reassess life. 'The family wanted me to come home and we think we might go. Being somewhere without earthquakes is pretty important. It definitely has affected me and it will be with me for the rest of my life. But I'm very pleased to be alive and very pleased my lottery ticket wasn't up. It's pure chance but I'm very grateful to be here. I'm one of the very lucky ones.'

FOOTNOTE: Jim and his family moved back to England later in July 2011.

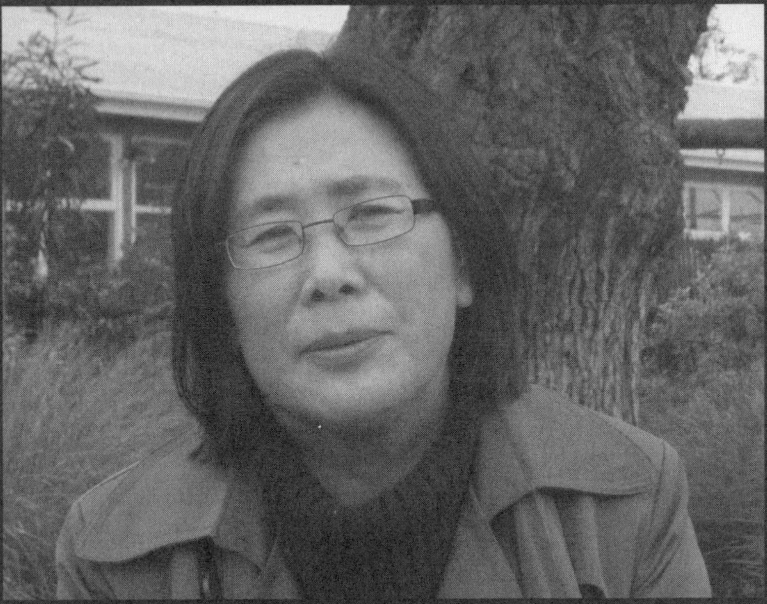

14

QING TANG

*'I remember looking up and thinking,
Wow. There is a way out. Blue sky.'*

THE CHRISTCHURCH EARTHQUAKES of 4 September 2010 and 22 February 2011 were not the first major earthquakes Qing Tang had experienced. She was a 14-year-old in Beijing, China, when a 7.8 magnitude earthquake in Yangtang, around 140 km from Beijing, killed about 250,000 people. She spent two months living in a tent before she was allowed back to her apartment building.

A nurse by training, Qing came to New Zealand in 1988 to be with her husband, an acupuncture practitioner. They separated in 1995 after having two girls, who at the time of the February earthquake were 19 and 21.

Qing's childhood was passed in a series of foster homes. A parcel child, she calls it. Her mother was killed in 1966 in a random act in Beijing during the Cultural Revolution and her father, who was an English graduate, was sent to a labour camp after an English journal was found at his house. He was not released until 1978. Her grandfather, Tang Wuyuan, was a military doctor and ended up vice-mayor of Wuhan, now a sister city of Christchurch. A democracy supporter, he was eventually declared a counter-revolutionary and killed, also in 1966.

Christchurch was a new beginning after the collapse of her family in China. She studied psychology and education at the University of Canterbury, obtaining two degrees, and became a counsellor. She had been working as a counsellor for Relationship Services for about three years and on 22 February was at a cultural awareness meeting with other counsellors in the CTV building in Madras Street. The session was headed by Louise Tankersley, who had brought along her eight-month-old baby.

Qing was sitting on her office chair against an internal wall looking towards Cashel Street when the earthquake struck. 'I was sitting down on a chair with wheels. I was thrown to the side and there was no time to protect myself. I felt a big push like an aeroplane crash. A big bang. I didn't have a second to think about what was happening. The door protected me. Then I saw the pink batts and big posts and frames. There was heavy dust and I found it hard to breathe. In front of me was Louise's baby. My first thought was, *Is baby OK?* I started to cough.'

Construction workers James Askew and Lenny Fortune had been working on top of a scissor lift on the Cashel and Madras Street corner of the building and had to jump from the platform as cinder blocks started raining down on them. They ran for their lives and when they looked back they were aghast to see the building flattened. 'We knew there were people there. We could hear them moving and making noises and we just had to get there,' James told reporters a few days afterwards. 'We pulled a bit of iron out of the way and there were people standing there. One of them had a baby. The baby was passed down a couple of people and then the mother came out. A few more people came out. They were absolutely astonished,' he said.

One of those astonished survivors was Qing. 'I remember looking up and thinking, *Wow. There is a way out. Blue sky.*'

Everyone wanted to save the baby, who was screaming. 'All I was thinking about was the baby and then I was just thinking about getting down step by step. I was just focusing on one thing. Forget about all other things. I heard people screaming but I just looked at one step at a time. Lots of screaming and other noises but I refused to process it.'

She says she lost sense of time and has no idea how long it took her to get down from the gap in the rubble in which they had landed. She remembers she was hugged by Louise and by a man who said his daughter was inside 'but it was like he was talking a foreign language'.

'I was in total shock. I followed people to Latimer Square, just doing as I was told.'

It was not until later she realised she had a very badly bruised arm and side and was unable to hold things with her left hand. Her first thought was to find her children. Her second was for her thesis which she had been working on for three years and which she had intended to hand in to the university the next day, her day off. It was on her laptop at home. 'Everything else I don't mind. It's replaceable,' she says.

Her 19-year-old daughter Lizzy (not her real name) was working in a fashion shop in Cashel Street. Qing tried several routes to get to the shop but was turned back by police. About 2.30 p.m. she decided to walk to her home in Redwood about 12 km away. 'I hadn't thought about being lucky to be alive. I wasn't really aware. Everything was dust, smoke, ambulance, screaming and people with blood on their face. All I thought was that I had to find my daughter.'

'Everything was dust, smoke, ambulance, screaming and people with blood on their face. All I thought was that I had to find my daughter.'

As she tried to get to Cashel Street, a couple told her the Christchurch Cathedral had collapsed and for the first time she realised something very serious had happened. 'I tell myself to walk and see how far you can go. Don't pay attention to anything else.'

When she arrived at Kilmore Street she approached a woman in a car and asked her to drive her home. Qing was still so dazed she was not aware people were in the back seat with her until later. Dropped off near her home, she found she didn't know what to say to her rescuer. 'I couldn't say what I wanted to say,' she says.

With her keys still in the wreckage of the CTV building, she was unable to get into her undamaged home and went to a neighbour's house, where she suddenly realised she was thirsty and cold. It was now 5 p.m. and she had still had no word from her children. Later, when she returned to her own house, her daughter Jess (not her real name) had arrived and they startled each other. 'I said, "It's me. I'm here."'

Jess had earlier received a phone call from Lizzy, who after the earthquake had run from her shop to the CTV building and saw it for herself. Believing nobody could have survived, she rang her sister to say their mother was dead. With Qing very definitely alive, Jess immediately rang Lizzy with the happy news, but Lizzy did not believe her and was only convinced when she spoke to Qing herself. Lizzy had already called a family friend in China to say her mother had died. As no information was available, the family friend went to two fortune tellers. Both said Qing was alive but she should leave Christchurch.

In the days after the earthquake Qing still felt shocked and overwhelmed. She packed a bag for a quick departure and wherever she went in the house, she carried it with her. She could not talk to people and when she met people from her Dutch Reform Church, she burst into tears and could not stop crying. When people said hello, she could not respond. She went to organise a new credit card and her inability to handle simple details made her realise she needed to leave Christchurch for a while. She booked tickets for herself and her daughters to visit family in Sydney. 'I needed to get my head to operate and I thought it does not work here in Christchurch. The knowledge and training was not there. In Sydney it was better. I realised something had happened to me.'

Three days later they returned very early in the morning and got up to find Qing's church friends had given her garden a complete makeover. 'It just blew me away. It was so comforting.'

Over the next few weeks the best therapy for her was appreciating small things, she says.

'Being in the garden and hearing the birds sing gave me a sense of calm and was very grounding. It helped me feel I was not on the fifth floor. I was trying to focus on just now. Touching the grass,

Before she wanted to get the job finished, whereas now she remembers she may not and tries to enjoy the work itself.

cooking a simple meal and trying to let go. I didn't watch television.'

Six weeks after the earthquake she went back to work and realised she needed a project to take her mind off her ordeal. She decided to do a family history.

Qing still dislikes confined spaces although she has deliberately gone to the movies and parked in underground carparks to gradually expose herself to the things she fears. She appreciates people more, she says. 'Now if I say goodbye, I don't do it like I did. I didn't see the kindness and generosity before. Because of my life I have been independent so it was a shock to find out people were so sad [when they thought] that I had died. I was so surprised.'

Her ordeal has made her enjoy the process of projects, such as studying, rather than the outcome. Before she wanted to get the job finished, whereas now she remembers she may not and tries to enjoy the work itself.

Qing does not see much point in asking why she survived. More useful and productive questions for her are what she has learned from the experience and where to from here.

'We all have stories about something that happened. The question is how we use those stories. What have I learned?'

Life is a mixed bag that unfortunately will often contain some random tragedy, she says. 'It is not for me to understand why. The universe is this big and I am just a tiny part of it. I am not demanding an answer from God. But I do believe if God did not take me this time, there is something else for me to do.'

The experience, she says, has probably made her a better counsellor because, 'I can relate to people from the inside.'

Ed Post (left) and Gordon Cullen.

15

ED POST
GORDON CULLEN

'It was an ordinary old working day in the corporate world with meetings and discussions and then all of sudden it was survival.'

ACCOUNTANT ED POST and Forsyth Barr investment adviser Gordon Cullen looked out of their fifth-floor boardroom and saw a sight which both shocked them and settled the question they both had. From the window they could see the dust still rising from the collapsed Pyne Gould Corporation building in Cambridge Terrace. Their building, the well-known 17-storey Forsyth Barr building on the corner of Armagh and Colombo Streets, was still standing but, unnervingly, its stairwell had collapsed, leaving them trapped. No doubt they would eventually be rescued but neither were prepared to wait when so many of the old certainties had collapsed around them.

Gordon had worked in the building for about nine years and Ed, formerly a partner of accountancy firm Duns Ltd, had moved his new firm into the building four days before Christchurch's September quake, after which the building seemed largely undamaged. 'You wouldn't have known an earthquake had happened from the state of the building,' says Ed, a father of three.

The stairwell had dropped about 25 mm and had come out from the wall but engineers green-stickered the building and in February workers were in the process of plastering the gaps and repainting.

Ed and Gordon are trustees of the Gestalt Institute and were having a trustee meeting in Ed's office on the fifth floor with fellow trustees Ian Rae, Nicola Holmes and Brenda Levin when the shaking and rumbling started on 22 February. A big cabinet containing books and files fell over and 'just about wiped out' Ed, who was still sitting in his chair. The case hit the side of his lower leg and gave him a nasty graze. Gordon, who has three children under 10, saw papers start to float across the room but Ed had other things on his mind.

> '**I just thought, This is huge. Oh my God. How many people have died?**'

'I remember looking at Nicola and thinking this is getting big and we were obviously thinking the same thing. I ducked down. I must have missed something for a while because the next thing I remember is getting up and looking at the PGC building.'

Gordon says he went for the underside of the table as well but every available space was taken. He walked around, telling himself not to stand in certain places and trying to stay on his feet. The first punch was the worst. When the shaking stopped they looked out the window to see the alarming sight of the collapsed PGC building. They saw dust engulfing the streets and heard the wailing of sirens. 'That just went on and on. It stays in your head, that noise,' says Ed.

From his vantage point Gordon could see people he knew on the street and a crowd streaming out of the 20-storey PricewaterhouseCoopers building in Armagh Street. 'I just thought, *This is huge. Oh my God. How many people have died?*'

Ian Rae and Ed went to check the stairs, only to find a dark chasm where their escape route should have been. Ed found out very quickly that Ian was an experienced caver and was therefore familiar with ropes and getting into and out of small gaps. 'He was thinking about going down. We could nearly jump on them from where we were because they had concertinaed down to the fourth floor. I said, "We are not going that way."'

Neither of them knew the stairwell between the fifteenth and seventeenth floors had survived the first shake and was still suspended, albeit precariously, above. 'It is a bit disconcerting,' says Gordon with typical Kiwi understatement, 'to realise there were still stairs hanging above ready to come down. You looked up but all you could see was dust floating around.'

As it happened, the remnant of the stairs came down with a huge bang at 2.45 p.m. but Ed was so busy concentrating on other things that he didn't hear them fall.

As they looked into the vacant space they heard someone calling from the seventh floor. It was Gabriel Marsden, an apprentice carpenter for the construction firm AW Interiors. He had been unscrewing furniture on the floor with another worker, who had gone downstairs to get a spanner, leaving Gabriel alone when the earthquake hit. They were working on the new fit-out of the floor for Forsyth Barr, which had relocated to the twelfth floor of the building while the work was done.

One of Ed's staff members, Diana Li-Stacey, suddenly came forward with the fire hose and asked if it was any good to anyone. Ian could see the potential and explained to Gabriel how to use the fire hose to come down the two floors. With Gabriel safely down, they then stood around wondering what to do. They could get out or wait for rescue. Ed and Gordon say there was no argument about the best course of action.

'My thoughts were to get out. I thought, because the PGC building had gone, it had escalated to a level we hadn't seen. So I just thought, *Let's just make some progress. We can't sit here.* We had no communication. We were on our own and were fortunate we only had to go two floors,' Gordon says.

'We never thought we would wait to get rescued. It never entered my head,' says Ed. 'It was, *How do we get out of here?* The stairs did not give us a lot of confidence. We all just wanted to get out.'

'I would do it again. Even if we had to go all the way to the ground from the fifth floor,' Gordon says.

The question was how far the fire hose would go down and when it was reeled out they found it was easily long enough to reach the carpark roof on the east side of the building and only two floors down. But first they had to smash the window and Ed, with a tea towel over his head to protect his eyes from possible splinters, used a coat stand to smash the initial hole in the safety glass. To protect the fire hose, they placed a cushion on the window ledge.

The only other office on the floor was the Consular Office of Japan, in which Shoichi Kawai, the consul, was alone but did not want to leave. 'It was a classic,' says Gordon. 'We had absolutely no gear and next minute out comes this little Japanese man with a helmet and full visibility vest, all ready to go. Then he just went back into his office.'

Ed says they checked on him before they all abandoned the building but he had locked his door. 'They started beating his door down and he unlocked it but he was not leaving until he had the say-so.'

They wrapped the hose around a couch to anchor it and some discussion followed about who should go first. Ed had decided to go last and Gordon put his hand up. 'I just free-styled down. The hands got a bit hot and I remember just before I went over the edge, Brenda saying something like, "I'm not happy. I don't want you going."'

Gordon, who was out of the building by 1.45 p.m., says everyone was a bit traumatised but handled the ordeal extremely well. No-one panicked. The idea was for the first person out to get a ladder so the rest could climb down without resorting to the fire hose. Gordon's first problem was the roller door of the carpark was shut tight but as he went past the sensor, the door popped up enough for him to put a block under the gate and get out. 'I felt a lot safer on the ground,' says Gordon. 'When I ran along Armagh Street I thought, *You beauty* out of relief.'

He waved to Ed from Armagh Street and noticed the window was the only one smashed so far.

'Then he was off,' says Ed. 'We thought we just need to wait here and the ladder will be here shortly.'

Unbeknown to those left, Gordon was unable to return because once he was outside the cordon set up by fire and police officers, he was not allowed back to the building. He alerted officials to his colleagues' predicament but they had other priorities. Although he could do nothing more, Gordon stayed in Victoria Square for at least an hour.

Those remaining on the fifth floor decided to get on with the evacuation but instead of people free-styling down the hose like

Gordon, they decided to tie the hose under each person's arms and lower them down. 'Ian did the knots which was quite good because I only know one knot,' says Ed. 'After we lowered Diana down, the Fire Service guys turned up and said, "Stay where you are. You are in the safest place." We were just sitting around and I said, "I think I would quite like to go out." We told the fire guys and they said it was at our own risk.'

While the men were working with the hose, Ed's other assistant, Jayne Belcher, went back to the office and came out with her bag and threw it out the window to Diana. It went straight through her hands and hit the carpark floor. 'What she had done was pull up the back-up disc from the office computer and put it in her bag. To have the forethought to do that was pretty amazing,' says Ed. The disc was undamaged and subsequently was a great help in enabling the office to get back on its feet quickly.

Ian went down last. 'He was down in about five seconds. It was a bit surreal because you've been through this experience and, well, what do we do now?'

Down on the ground they had lots of hugs. 'I missed out on the party,' Gordon says.

The rest of the building was evacuated by crane by 6 p.m. the same day and for Gordon and Ed, there was nothing for it but to go home; Gordon to West Melton and Ed to Avonhead. Their houses were, fortunately, undamaged.

Ed says he would not go back into the Forsyth Barr building as a tenant. 'I just don't trust that building because the stairs collapsed. My staff and probably my clients would not go back into a high rise.'

Months later Ed and Gordon went back to their respective floors to retrieve files. Gordon says his firm struggled to

> 'I just free-styled down. The hands got a bit hot and I remember just before I went over the edge, Brenda saying something like, "I'm not happy. I don't want you going."'

get volunteers to go back but Ed says his staff couldn't wait. They found a lot of dust, mouldy sandwiches and apples, with one exception. 'Diana was cooking herself a toasted sandwich when the earthquake struck and when she went back, the toasted sandwich was in the same place and there was nothing wrong with it. You could have eaten the bloody thing,' says Ed.

Gordon says he looks back on 22 February as a day which switched in a second. 'I look back and think it was an ordinary old working day in the corporate world with meetings and discussions and then all of sudden it was survival. People say it was a war zone but that was an exaggeration. But it was, *What do we do to get out?* You just had to look at the PGC and you knew there were deaths over there.'

FOOTNOTE: Stage 1 of the Expert Panel Report into the collapse of the Forsyth Barr building (built in 1988), released on 30 September 2011, notes the stairs collapsed on one side of the stairwell up to Level 14 and on the other side up to Level 15. The stairs were designed in a scissor arrangement. The panel concluded the main causes of collapse were the intensity and characteristics of the shaking and the possibility the seismic gaps at the lower supports were filled with material that restricted movement.

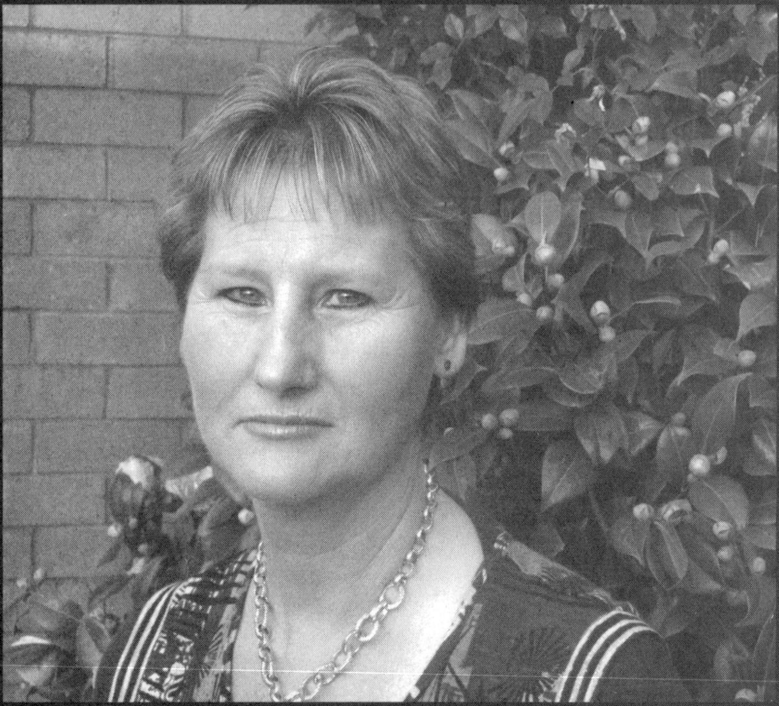

16

LYN REID

'I thought, Hell, I'm stuck; I'm going with the building.'

The *Press* building from Worcester Street with its collapsed third floor and toppled turret.

Holes had to be cut in the concrete roof of the *Press* building to gain access to trapped and injured.

Ian Reddington was trapped under this part of the collapsed roof of the *Press* building.

View of collapsed *Press* roof, looking towards the Hotel Grand Chancellor.

All that was left of the stairwell leading from the roof of the *Press* building down past the cafeteria.

Inside the *Press* cafeteria.

LYN REID LOOKED at her legs trapped under a hulking beam. She could hardly feel them. But worse than that, much worse, was her fear that the building was going down as it shuddered in the aftershocks. Her only thought was, *Get me out of here*. It would be hours before rescuers could fulfil her agonised wish.

Lyn was a familiar figure around the *Press* building. Always impeccably groomed, she had been cheerfully keeping the newspaper's cafeteria and kitchens clean and tidy for 11 years. She worked Mondays and Tuesdays, mainly for a bit of pocket money to supplement her husband Murray's earnings as an electrician, and enjoyed the job until the Boxing Day earthquake, a 4.9 magnitude aftershock, in 2010.

The northern wall of the historic part of the *Press* building, made of brick, was damaged in the 4 September quake and needed shoring up. After the repairs the building was declared safe by both the owner's engineers and independent engineers commissioned by *The Press* but Lyn had her doubts. 'I didn't like being in that building seeing the devastation in there. They kept saying it's safe but I had a feeling about that place. I wondered if we should be in there. Even coming back after the September quake was bad enough. I did hate it. I thought it's a job but did I really need to be here? Do I really want this?'

On 22 February she took the bus from Avondale to Cathedral Square and worked until the start of her lunch hour at midday. She had brought her own lunch, a filled roll, and sat down at one of the third-floor cafeteria's lacquered tables with the day's newspaper and a cup of tea. To the left was a wall of French doors along the north side of the building and an outside patio where people could sit and enjoy the sun. The table was near to the wall previously damaged in the September earthquake and subsequent aftershocks and Lyn had since avoided the area but time had allayed her fears and it was a pleasant spot to sit.

'I hadn't been sitting there for ages but that day I thought nothing more is going to happen. Tim [Cronshaw (Chapter 7)] was sitting in front of me. I thought it was just a tremor but when it didn't stop I said, "Bloody hell, get me out of here." I thought, *Where shall I go?* and Tim got up and I followed him. I thought, *Get away from doors and go under the beam because that should hold*. I hung onto Tim's shirt-tails. We were both looking at the stairwell. It was so quick and then I was looking at the sky. I was out in the open.'

She was pinned, with the concrete beam under which had she sought protection on both her legs. The roof of the building, which was essentially another concrete floor with tarseal on top, had tilted and fallen towards the east, opening up the part of the cafeteria where Lyn was trapped. The beam had caught her left leg above the knee inflicting a deep gash but more weight was on her right leg. She also had a cut to her head, which was bleeding, and her arm was dislocated from the shoulder.

She remained conscious and found her face close to Tim's feet, which were thrashing about as he tried to kick himself free. He didn't realise it at the time but he came very close to kicking Lyn in the face and she worried she would lose a few teeth.

'I said, "Hey, I'm here." Tim was flat under this rubble and I was surprised he got out of there. Then I could see different people popping out. Someone gave me a hug and then disappeared. I thought, *Where did they come from?*'

Tim remembers Lyn being in terrible pain but Lyn says she was more scared than anything because she thought the building was going to come down. 'With the aftershocks I thought, *Here we go*. You just think of the [Twin] Towers and you think that is going to happen. I thought, *Hell, I'm stuck; I'm going with the building.* I was terrified. I said, "Don't leave me here. Just get me out of here." I just put up with the pain, I think. I just blacked it all out. If Tim had decided to go I would not have blamed him, but he didn't. I wouldn't have said, "Why did you leave me?" We were all scared. People were crying and screaming and yelling and I could hear the rescue guys and the helicopters and I thought, *Far out.* I didn't think I would get out of there. Whatever they did, they couldn't move that beam. My injuries were so serious, I did think I wasn't going to survive this.'

Her head was bleeding but it wasn't painful and she could hear Len McKenzie, the building supervisor, who had been at another cafeteria table, and Ian Reddington, a subeditor, who was pinned by his hand, calling out. Lyn remained trapped for about three hours with each aftershock putting more pressure on her injured legs. She couldn't feel her toes and a numbness took over, although she remained conscious. She went into shock and was shaking.

Time seemed to take on a different meaning up on the roof, she says. 'It just doesn't make sense. I couldn't believe I was up there for three hours.'

She remembers Tim, who had promised to stay with her, saying he had to go and also the arrival on the scene of George Piper, the *Press*'s maintenance man. 'It was not a big wrench when Tim said he had to go. No. I was just so grateful he stayed as long as he did. You just wanted some other human contact, someone talking to you saying, "I'm not going to leave you here all on your own." The prospect of dying alone was pretty awful.

'George didn't know my name and kept calling me something else. I said, "For God's sake. My name is Lyn." But they were all wonderful. They just came so quickly. Somebody was up there almost all the time but I expected the worst. When you saw the sky and all the roof gone, I didn't think people could survive.'

Lyn would often have a chat with Adrienne Lindsay, who died in the building, when Adrienne came in for morning tea and lunchtime. 'She was a very bright girl. Full of life.'

Lyn also knew Stacey Reeves, 22, another finance section staff member who was sitting close to Adrienne when the roof collapsed. A model in her spare time, Stacey was trapped with a huge weight on her legs. Her head was also crushed. Both her legs were amputated. After fighting for her life in intensive care in Christchurch Hospital for many days, she pulled through and married her boyfriend, Nick Herbert, in early June.

Although several attempts were made to relieve the pressure on Lyn, it was not until a crane arrived that rescuers were able to raise the beam and get Lyn to hospital. Although she couldn't see the crane because of something shielding her head, she felt the pressure go off her legs and with it came a great sense of relief to be getting off the building. 'Once in the ambulance they started working on me. I was just so glad to get out of the building. They said, "We will have to cut your clothes off," and I said, "Do what you like."'

Lyn spent a very unhappy week in Christchurch Hospital. Her legs were not broken but she had large dents, abrasions, blistering and puncture wounds. Two days after the earthquake, her hair was being washed and a large cut requiring 12 staples was discovered. She can't remember any severe pain but found the aftershocks, as experienced in her hospital bed on an upper floor, too much to take after her ordeal. About a week after she was admitted, an aftershock prompted a near breakdown.

'I was screaming and crying, the building was rocking around so much and I said, "Just get me out of here please." So within the hour I was out of there. I just packed my things up, came back and the ambulance was waiting for me. In Burwood Hospital I was on a single level and I had my own room. It was heavenly. I had a television on the wall and could see outside. I did not need psychological help. I wasn't traumatised. I just didn't like the feeling of the aftershocks.'

After three weeks in either Christchurch or Burwood Hospitals,

Lyn, who has two adult daughters, returned to her liveable but damaged home near the Avon River for more recuperation. She does exercises to strengthen her arm and although her legs are still swollen, her walking gets a little better each day. She still keeps busy and her house and garden are immaculate. 'I loved my gardening and walking and it has just slowed me down. I'm not one to sit down all day but I just can't wait to get back to the way I was.'

Lyn and Murray are considering some major life changes as a result of the earthquake. Their house is cracked and no longer level but eventually they want to sell and move away from the seaside suburb because Lyn is worried about a tsunami. She says she is reminded about her experience every time an aftershock hits but does not have nightmares and the memories are not traumatic. She will not, however, ever work in a multi-storey building again.

'You don't know if that is the last one or not. I am on tenterhooks all the time because you just don't know. I can't relax. Where do you go? Where do you move to be safe? We have the Alpine fault and all the fault lines around us. I did not worry about these things before. I didn't think they would happen in my lifetime. You can't relax, not truly relax. Even when we go to a mall, we park out in the open. Inside the mall, one level is OK but I don't like being in there for too long. I know it's not in your control any more what's above you.'

She and Murray were on the verge of buying a four-wheel-drive vehicle before the earthquake and they intend to carry on with that plan and go for a holiday. Lyn is also keen on getting a little dog and the couple are planning a trip to Hawaii with friends. 'He is a golfer and I am a golf widow. I like gardening, walking, reading. There are four mates who play and the wives just do other things.'

Lyn says she doesn't worry as much about the small things in life now. 'Not the frivolous things like chattels. They don't matter. I think of other people who might need a hand. Life is too short to worry about little things.'

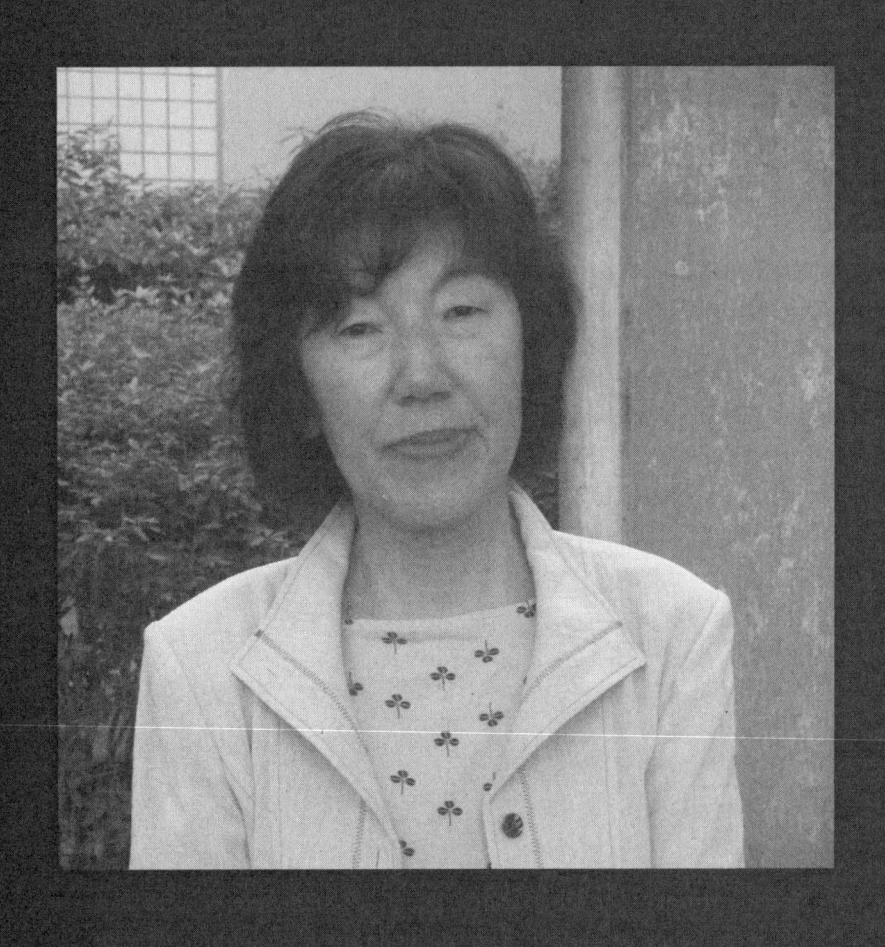

17

HIROKO SATO

'My best friend was talking to me, saying,
"I can't breathe. I can't breathe."'

AS HIROKO SATO lay in the darkness next to her best friend Yoshiko Hirauchi, she prepared for death. 'I decide in the darkness that I die here. I was happy all my life. I am going to die,' the former administrator for the Toyama Police says.

But despite these feelings, she exhorted the injured Yoshiko to hang on. They had shared many moments throughout their lives but nothing like this.

A star graduate of the two-year English course at the Toyama College of Foreign Languages (TCFL), Hiroko was one of the 21 TCFL students and two staff who came to Christchurch for the three-week course at King's Education in the CTV building. The mother of an adult son and daughter, she wanted to learn English so she could travel with Yoshiko, a retired school teacher. The two had been friends since high school and had continued their friendship through university, marriage, children and work. Neither of their husbands enjoyed travel so the fit and active pair set off on adventures, including climbing Mt Fuji, by themselves.

Hiroko had booked to go on the college's Christchurch trip in 2010 but her father-in-law died and she had to stay home. 'I went with the younger ones. I loved New Zealand before I come to this school, so I was looking forward to it very much. I was looking forward to going with Yoshiko very much.'

She did not know all the students in the group well but, like their teachers, felt

> 'I loved New Zealand before I come to this school, so I was looking forward to it very much. I was looking forward to going with Yoshiko very much.'

they were cheerful, funny, hardworking and serious about studying. 'I always feel they are the same as my friends. They treated me like a mother. I wanted to encourage them. If they had worries or problems, I gave them advice like a mother about school and boyfriends and girlfriends.'

She knew Christchurch had had an earthquake in September but had been reassured by her New Zealand teacher, David Horsley (Chapter 5). After all, no-one had died.

When the group arrived in Christchurch on 19 February, her homestay host was Rose Porter, in Parklands, and her two cats. Rose did a dry run of the bus trip to the King's Education school with Hiroko and they bought a metro card. They drove up to the Summit Road to see the view and spent the rest of the weekend making zucchini pickle.

On the class walk on Monday, Hiroko enjoyed the beautiful day and blue sky. They went to the Arts Centre and visited the Great Hall with its spectacular stained glass windows. On Tuesday she and Yoshiko ended up in different classes and when they met up in the cafeteria at lunchtime, Yoshiko had saved a seat for her.

> **'My foot was twisted and I felt someone correcting it. After a while someone pulled my legs and my arm became free and I was dragged out by my legs.'**

'My class was longer than other classes and I was late. I began to eat lunch and then the earthquake started. I was sitting at the end of the table beside my best friend and I went under the table. I remember thinking I have to get under the table, but can't remember falling. Then it was dark and I couldn't see anything. No light at all.'

When the shaking stopped she could hear voices. 'My best friend was talking to me, saying, "I can't breathe. I can't breathe." I told her to keep fighting, to keep trying. I couldn't touch her in the small space and I couldn't move my right arm or left leg. My face was down and I could breathe a little. After that the smoke came. My friend says about the rescuers, "Please hurry up. Hurry up." After that I didn't hear her.'

Eventually she heard the sounds of rescue equipment and knew the rescue had started. 'I don't know how soon I was rescued but it was probably between 5 and 6 p.m. I did not feel pain. I had a few cuts and scratches and a friction burn and I wanted to move the weight of the rubble. But I didn't notice the pain.'

During the rescue she found someone on her leg. It was Yoshiko. 'I thought she was alive because the body was warm. My foot was twisted and I felt someone correcting it. After a while someone pulled my legs and my arm became free and I was dragged out by my legs. I could see light and could see rescuers' faces. They put me on a stretcher and I was carried out. I could see the other buildings were OK and I was shocked. I said thank you to the rescuers and one said, "Well done." *Why?* I thought to myself.'

She arrived at Christchurch Hospital and her clothes were cut off. Her right ankle was stitched and a burn treated. She could not move her right arm but a doctor said it would come right in three days. Three months later, and after intensive physiotherapy, the arm is slowly getting better. She still has trouble holding things and some parts of her hand are still numb.

She was worried sick about Yoshiko and no-one could find her in the hospital. Unfortunately Hiroko's host family had its own problems. Rose's daughter Emma (Chapter 4) was trapped in the collapsed PGC building in Cambridge Terrace and although she was rescued about 8 p.m., Rose was in no position to support Hiroko.

About midnight Hiroko was told she had to go home. 'I was very surprised. I said, "Please let me stay."' She had no clothes, no money and could not contact Rose. She was at a complete loss what to do when a nurse, Chris Scott, invited her to come home with her. 'I stayed at her home. I felt in her I had met an angel.'

Chris's house was already full. Her son Reuben was away on camp but she had her parents and her mother-in-law staying because of earthquake damage to their homes. 'So many people in Chris's house,' Hiroko says. 'They were all in bed and said hello. I was surprised it was such a big family. They were very nice and very kind. I couldn't go back to Rose's house and she brought my suitcase so next day I could wear my clothes.'

Hiroko slept in Reuben's bed and next morning got into the swing of life in an earthquake city. The Scott family could not use their shower and had to boil their water. They used a bucket for a toilet. Chris washed Hiroko's dust-caked hair the next day using what water they had.

Reuben, when he returned from camp, and the Scott's 16-year-old daughter Rebecca tried to make Hiroko feel at home and distract her from the sadness she felt about her friend and the students who were killed or injured. 'Rebecca showed me a hedgehog. I couldn't open my pill bottle and Reuben would open it for me and sometimes I forgot the pill and he brought the pill. I could not write and he would write numbers for me and, at the airport on the way back to Japan, he helped keep the media away. So he was like a bodyguard, nurse and secretary.'

A rumour had circulated that Yoshiko had been injured and sent to an Auckland hospital. TCFL teacher Susan Urakami, who had arrived from Toyama to help, returned from Auckland with no news. Any hope of Yoshiko still being alive dwindled quickly.

Five days after the earthquake, Hiroko moved to Methven, where the Japanese families were staying, to help a surviving student who was traumatised and needed someone with her. She moved in with Yuki Matsuta, who runs a Japanese restaurant in Methven, and when he delivered food to the families at the lodge she went along in the back of the van so she could talk to the other group.

She returned to Japan on 3 March and was touched by the large turnout to say goodbye. She doesn't know how to thank the Scott family enough and hopes to see them again on another trip to Christchurch. She wants to know why the CTV building collapsed and feels more guilty than lucky.

'Before Yoshiko went she broke her elbow when she slipped on the ice and had her arm in a sling before the trip. If I didn't go, maybe she didn't go. She wanted to go with me. I didn't recommend for her to go with me but she wanted to come. Even though it was hard she wanted to go. I feel guilty because I am older than the younger students. I have lived a long time already, so I didn't need to live any more. So many outstanding students passed away. Not me.

'I feel guilty because I am older than the younger students. I have lived a long time already, so I didn't need to live any more . . . I feel empty in my life and mind because I have lost my best friend.'

'I feel empty in my life and mind because I have lost my best friend. We were very busy because we both worked and last spring she had retired, so from now we will spend many times together. We made plans to travel and we planned to go to the mountains. I don't know if I can enjoy life again but I have to have many rich experiences because I want to talk about them to my best friend when I meet her again. I want to go to Christchurch once more and want to meet Rose and the Scott family so I have to improve my English skills.

'That day I lost my best friend, I met the best family in New Zealand. They are the best.'

Top: Rochelle Prattley and Glenn Prattley.
Above: Glenn with his partner Kelsey Moore and their daughter Taneysha, who were both killed in the earthquake. COURTESY OF GLENN PRATTLEY

18

ROCHELLE PRATTLEY
GLENN PRATTLEY

'All I heard was the sirens. I blocked out the rest of the noise and was screaming for someone to help us.'

ONE OF THE MOST dangerous places to be in the 22 February earthquake in Christchurch was in the drop zone of the façade of any old brick, two-storey building in the central city. Many of the deaths and injuries were caused by brick and masonry façades tumbling onto footpaths, roads and verandas. People in cars were crushed and verandas collapsed under the weight of the rubble, trapping those underneath.

The danger, which in retrospect seems eminently foreseeable, took a terrible toll on Mosgiel brother and sister Glenn and Rochelle Prattley. Both received broken bones and crush injuries but much worse was the death of Glenn's partner, Christchurch-born Kelsey Moore, and their baby Taneysha, only five weeks old at the time.

Glenn had met Kelsey through the social network website Bebo, a sort of early Facebook, and the pair had been corresponding for about a year before Glenn moved up to Christchurch to look for work. Kelsey was the oldest of five children, was unhappy at school and home, and moved in with Glenn, in his central city flat in Edgeware, when she was still 17. They experienced the 4 September earthquake together, with Glenn thinking she was shaking the bed. She had their baby Taneysha on 17 January, a day before Glenn's twenty-eighth birthday. Taneysha was two weeks premature and weighed in at just over 2.5 kg. She had dark hair and blue eyes.

Glen, who worked on dairy farms around the South Island after he left school, found he took naturally to first-time fatherhood. 'I pretty much loved being a hands-on dad. I just loved everything about it and Taneysha was a really easy baby. Everyone said so. We had lots of cuddles and Kelsey loved being a mother. Taneysha was pretty much always smiling and feeding well.'

Kelsey was not the greatest cook so Glen did most of the cooking. 'She was quiet and she always put everybody else before herself,' Glenn says of Kelsey. 'She was really happy to be pregnant because she had been told she couldn't have kids. She was brilliant with Taneysha and wanted to do a childcare course by correspondence. I was going to get back into dairy farming.'

Kelsey's parents were not happy with the relationship but Glenn says, given the chance, he could have showed them he was a good partner and father. Glenn and Rochelle are also part of a large family, having two brothers and a sister. They are keen rodeo followers and their older brother Jeff was Rookie Cowboy of the Year when he was only 14. Their father was a high-country shepherd for 13 years and continued with rodeo until he was in his thirties.

Rochelle went to Queen's High School in Dunedin and her studies focused on child development. After school she studied social work and childcare at Otago Polytechnic and in 2010 she spent five months working in Chicago in a camp for children and adults with cerebral palsy. After Taneysha's birth she went to Christchurch to lend a hand with the new baby. 'She was a very happy-go-lucky little girl. She was very content and never cried.'

> 'All I heard was the sirens. I blocked out the rest of the noise and was screaming for someone to help us.'

With two mothers in the house she and Kelsey eventually clashed and Rochelle decided to go home and look for work in childcare or care of the elderly. She booked a bus ticket for 22 February. On the day of the earthquake, Glenn, who had not found a permanent job, told Rochelle he would walk her to the bus depot in Worcester Street, in central Christchurch. Kelsey and Taneysha came for the outing. They walked as a group to the depot to drop off Rochelle's suitcase and then carried on to the Countdown

Supermarket in Moorhouse Avenue to get some baby formula.

After the supermarket they walked back along Manchester Street and at the Lichfield intersection Kelsey took Taneysha from her stroller because she was grizzling and carried her. Glenn carried on ahead with the stroller. When the ground started to shake they were on the footpath outside the former Ruben Blades hairdressing shop, which was closed because of damage in the September earthquake. Its glass front windows were still intact.

'It was kind of like someone had pushed us,' says Rochelle. 'I yelled to Glenn, "What's happening?" Kelsey and Taneysha were about two or three metres behind us. Glenn pushed me out of the way because there was a concrete thing coming straight for my head. I'm sure that saved my life.'

The façade of the building had fallen on the concrete veranda overhead, which folded back and crashed down, throwing Rochelle and Glenn through the Ruben Blades salon window. Miraculously they were not badly cut, but the back edge of the veranda and part of a wall landed on Rochelle's right foot and on both of Glenn's legs, trapping them. Rochelle landed on her back and Glenn, who was right beside her, was in a kneeling position with the rubble on the back of his legs, leaving him unable to lean forward. They were lying in the shop among the paraphernalia of a hair salon, including curlers and hair straighteners.

'We could not see outside and I was just hoping someone would come and get us out,' says Rochelle. 'We didn't know how bad it was outside. All I heard was the sirens. I blocked out the rest of the noise and was screaming for someone to help us. We didn't have any idea of what had happened to Kelsey and Taneysha. I remember telling Glenn we were going to die. I was in a lot of pain. Glenn was really worried about Kelsey and Taneysha and talking about them all the time.'

A broken bone had come through Glenn's left leg and he was also in severe pain. When he moved he could feel the bone rubbing.

'There was quite a bit going through my mind,' he says. 'Rochelle was saying we were going to die, so I had to stay as calm as possible and I said to Rochelle, "Don't even think like that." She had a concrete slab on her stomach, which we tried to get off. I couldn't see Kelsey and Taneysha and didn't know what had happened to them.'

They looked up at the swaying building and were convinced it would crash down on them in the aftershocks. A paramedic, police and some passers-by arrived after about 30 minutes and managed to get under the collapsed veranda to where Rochelle and Glenn were pinned. Although a digger was available to move the rubble it was decided that was too dangerous and that car jacks would have to be used to lift the wall off Rochelle and Glenn. It took three hours to free Rochelle and Glenn was not extracted for another three hours after Rochelle. It is believed Kelsey and Taneysha died instantly.

Rochelle's foot swelled up like a balloon as soon as the wall came off it and the pain increased dramatically. She was taken to a triage centre in Moorhouse Avenue and spent the night at the home of a doctor working at the centre. Rochelle tried to find out about Kelsey and Taneysha all evening. She managed to sleep a little between the shakes during the night and next day the doctor took her for an X-ray before her parents arrived to take her back to Mosgiel. Her foot was painful but she had no idea how serious the injury was until she went to Dunedin Hospital. 'I thought I just needed to go in for a check-up but I didn't get out of there for six weeks.' She needed several operations and skin grafts.

Glenn doesn't remember much about the day after he saw Rochelle being taken from the building as the painkillers he was given 'put me on another planet'. 'When I was in the hospital I was out in the corridor and asking everyone where my partner and daughter were. I wasn't getting any answers. After a while I got really angry. I said, "Look if you are not going to tell me, I will crawl out of here to find them." They said, "We will try and get some information and get back to you."'

Rochelle kept on to Red Cross and their brother Jeff and sister Renee rang hospitals around the country in an effort to find Glenn's partner and baby. Renee eventually brought a camera into the hospital and filmed Glenn making a plea for information which was broadcast on TV3 on Thursday night (24 February, the second day after the quake).

> Losing his partner and their baby was so overwhelming he still struggles to describe his reaction. 'There are just no words for it. I'm not sure I'll ever get over it.'

Glenn already suspected the worst, although his hopes had been raised when Rochelle and Renee were told, on the day after the quake, that Kelsey and Taneysha were in Starship Hospital in Auckland. Unfortunately that hope was to be dashed when other information was provided.

On Saturday 26 February, when he knew his partner and baby were dead, Glenn was flown to Dunedin Hospital and eventually ended up in a room with his sister. He would remain there for three weeks and was discharged a day before Kelsey's and Taneysha's funeral in Christchurch.

The Prattley family drove to Christchurch to attend the funeral, which they felt was overshadowed by tensions surrounding Glenn and Kelsey's relationship. What should have been a healing affair became another source of grief, Glenn says. He wants to hold his own memorial service for Kelsey and Taneysha.

Glenn is still angry it took almost two weeks before he knew for sure that Kelsey and Taneysha had been found. He had to provide a DNA sample before Taneysha could be formally identified. Losing his partner and their baby was so overwhelming he still struggles to describe his reaction. 'There are just no words for it. I'm not sure I'll ever get over it.'

Four months after the quake, the injuries suffered by the brother and sister still hamper their lives. Rochelle goes to a fracture clinic each week and might face further operations to straighten her foot.

Her days are 'kind of boring', she says. She still hopes to get work caring for the elderly or children.

At one stage Rochelle blamed herself for the deaths of Kelsey and the baby, because if she and Kelsey had not argued, she would not have gone home and they wouldn't have been in town on the day of the earthquake. Glenn tells her it is not her fault. As Glenn continues with physiotherapy to help him straighten his left leg, which was mended with a plate, he believes he is slowly coming right and when he can walk well, he hopes to go back to dairy farming.

In the aftermath of their ordeal, Rochelle and Glenn say they look at life differently. Rochelle has a new appreciation of the fragility of life, with little Taneysha having only a few weeks before she was taken. Glenn is haunted by the question of why he survived. 'It makes you respect everything you do have, but the same thought keeps crossing my mind, which is, *Why am I here and Taneysha and Kelsey aren't?*'

So far he hasn't come up with any answers.

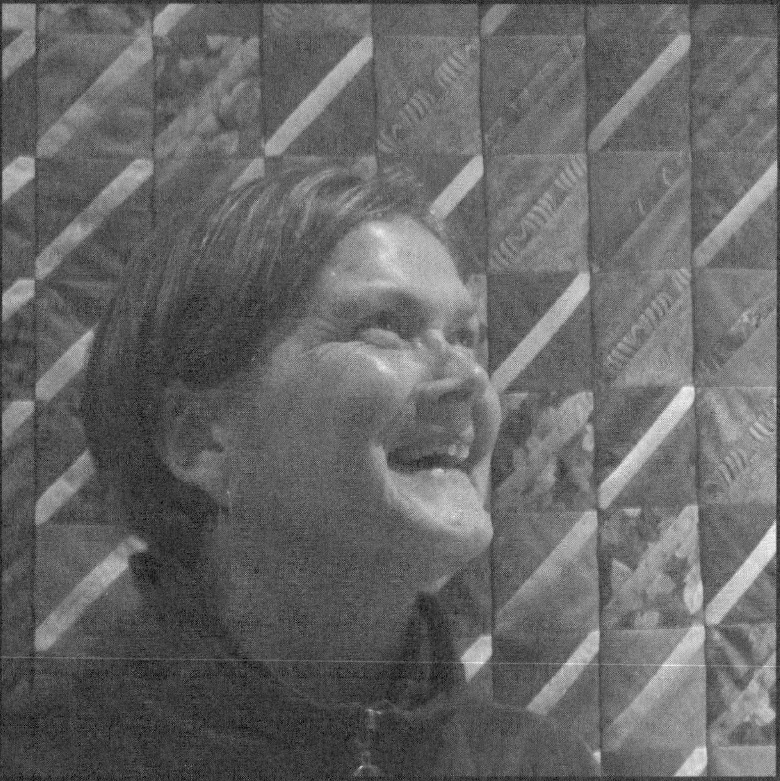

19

SUE SPIGEL

'I just started to laugh because the church
was trying to kill me.'

THE CHRISTCHURCH CATHEDRAL spire, which bursts from the Square like a spear, is one of the enduring symbols of Christchurch. To see it toppled in the earthquake of 22 February 2011 emphasised the crippling impact of the quake on the city. Its fall seemed symbolic of the loss of the city's heritage and grandeur in the tragic event. But for Sue Spigel it was more than a symbol. It was a death trap.

The renowned quilt maker, who was raised in Michigan and came to New Zealand about 20 years ago with husband Bob, a scientist, also became one of the many powerful images of the quake. Photographs taken of her emerging, broken and bloodied, from a Cathedral window were used by media around the world.

Her association with the Cathedral began in 2001 after she attended a memorial service for victims of the September 11 attack on the World Trade Center in New York. 'We had been in Christchurch for about twenty years but I always felt somewhat of a stranger and it was something about going into that cathedral and hearing the music and the words and I finally felt like I was home. Where I had come from was appreciated and local people mourned for the Americans. I liked that it was a public place to mourn the dead and it sort of was like a meeting house and gathering place for all these different cultures and people. A place where they celebrate and have music and art and people trying to make a difference.'

She became artist-in-residence in the Cathedral in 2007, making banners and other articles for the Cathedral and selling her quilts and other pieces through the Cathedral shop. Her room under the tower and spire was at the end of a stone stairway, so narrow the limestone would leave chalk on her sleeves.

'Twenty-two steps. Then you get up there and there is this beautiful little room and there are these leadlight stained glass windows and a little window seat. Being an introvert I thought it was wonderful to be in the Cathedral and in the centre of the city and to be able to watch what was going on but still be on my own and not be bothered by people. A lot of people did not know the room existed.'

The room looked out onto Christchurch's spectacular cenotaph and her view included a blind busker who played his flute just under her window most days. When youths taunted him, she wanted to go out and deal to them.

On the day of the earthquake, she arrived by car about 9.30 a.m. She had been working on a cope (a half-circle cape worn over the shoulders) for the Dean of Auckland and was looking forward to a good four-hour run to get the job finished. Sue started sewing when she was four, using her mother's machine to make dolls' clothes. After high school, she went on to complete a master's in Speech and Language Pathology and later taught herself quilt making which, as success followed success, became a new career.

> 'Then I thought, *I'm not ready to die.* I thought about my grandson . . . and how it would be such a big loss in my life not to see him grow up.'

The difficult sewing task was going well and she listened to the National Programme on the radio as she worked. 'I was enjoying myself. It was wonderful to listen to the National Programme and sew. Finally I got the last piece sewn together and ironed it out and it was just as flat as a pancake and looked really good.'

By then it was 12.50 p.m. and Sue thought about going for a cup of coffee but the radio programme *World Watch* had started and she sat in the window seat to listen. The window was open. 'There was this awful shake. It felt like someone had run into the wall below with a truck and I wanted to say, "Stop that." It began to get really violent and then I realised the ceiling and roof had separated from the walls because I could see it shaking up there and see daylight around the edges of the ceiling.

'I thought I should probably get under a desk and because the desk was further over I tried to stand up but just fell back down. There was no way I was going to get to that desk. I thought I could get down on my hands and knees but I couldn't move against the force of the shaking and I looked under the desk and thought that is where I should be.'

About five seconds later the tower started to break apart and a huge piece of masonry fell through the ceiling and landed on the desk, flattening it completely, cope and all. Then the floor gave way and Sue remained against the window, holding a stone support. 'Had I been under the desk that would have been it. I would have been killed immediately. I wouldn't have known what happened.'

Later, in hospital, she met an Australian couple who were in the cathedral below her room at the time of the earthquake. The man had pulled a large piece of wood from his leg and Sue believes it may well have come from the desk.

As the floor gave way so did the ceiling, and wood, bricks, stone and dirt rained down on Sue. 'I just kept looking at it. I got hit on the head by a brick and started to bleed because I felt this warm stuff going down my front, but nothing hurt. I had holes all over me from the nails (in the wood) and I thought *I could die in here*. I thought, *This is the sort of thing people die of*, and then I put my arms up over my head. Then everything went black when the rest of the tower fell. It was like a dust storm and it was completely black. I could hear people screaming and there was so much dirt and dust in the air.'

At first Sue was completely enveloped in rubble but she managed to extract her arms. 'Then I thought, *I'm not ready to die*. I thought about my grandson [Jacob, 22 months] and how it would be such a big loss in my life not to see him grow up. Then it was so peculiar. A friend had emailed me a sign which said, *Don't let worries kill you, let the church help*. I just started to laugh because the church was trying to kill me. Here I was in this life or death situation. The stuff that goes through your head is amazing. I was basically very calm. I felt like I was watching this happen to me; that I was watching a movie.'

Sue says she had the feeling she was going to be all right even though she was aware her arm was not working – it turned out to be badly broken – and she was trapped and desperately wanted to get out.

'I tried to push the boards off but I couldn't because there was so much stuff on top of them. I managed to use one arm and push myself up off the seat until I was sitting on the window sill and could get up high enough to pull my feet up. I lost one of my sandals. Once the dust cleared I tried calling out but I couldn't because the dust caught in my throat. Then I was sitting there in the window looking and I started waving and said, "Hello" and, "Can you please get me out of here?" I was half out the window. It was dramatic, and that was when the photo was taken.'

People were on the footpath and Cathedral staff, who had been in a meeting at the back of the church, were also there. 'They came out and they were all just standing there and looking and I remember looking at them. But they all just stood there. They were all in shock.'

Peter Beck, the charismatic dean of the Cathedral, talked to her from the ground and tried to ring her husband Bob, who at that time was trying to get home in his car. Peter was unable to get through.

'I just motored on,' says Bob, who felt the quake at the head of a queue of cars in Durham Street. 'I knew she had talked about coming home early. I thought she may be in the Cathedral or she may be home. I didn't know. I had a feeling she was probably in the Cathedral. She had talked about staying so she could go to Jacob's swimming lesson. I wasn't sure. I got to the start of Cashmere Hill and thought this quake was a lot worse and things were probably really bad in the city. I tried to use my cellphone. I thought, *I will go home and hope she is there*. I managed to get home and found it a mess. The dogs had run away and Sue wasn't there and I thought, *Oh shit.*

Bob tried calling the Cathedral and the police but with no success. Hours went by. 'I just damned that room and I knew she didn't like going up there after the first earthquake. Betsy [their daughter, who lives next door] came over and I wasn't in a good frame of mind. My son called from Japan. Then I lost it and started to cry.'

After Bob returned from looking for the dogs, the phone rang. Sue had spotted someone she knew in the hospital and asked her to call Bob. 'I got a bunch of stuff and got to the hospital and I was just amazed how nice the nurses were. There she was. Oh man, that was amazing. She started crying and I started crying. I thought she looked pretty good.'

Sue managed to get down from her Cathedral room with help from police officer Paul Martin, who had managed to requisition a long ladder and climb into the room where she was trapped. 'I stuck one foot out the window and this person outside grabbed my foot and put it on one rung after the other. I just so wanted to get out of there. I felt a lot of aftershocks. The only thing holding up the wall seemed to be three cables for earthquake strengthening. It felt like it was wobbling the whole time and it seemed like there was just one aftershock after another.'

Sue arrived at the hospital filthy and with a broken arm, a cut head and numerous puncture wounds and bruises to her body. She was cleaned up a bit and told to return in seven to ten days for an operation to her arm. Although water had been cut to her Governors Bay home, the local reservoir still had a little water and she was able to wash herself, although she couldn't have a bath until two days later, when Bob washed her hair. For the first couple of days all she did was sleep. Within a few days she was called in for her operation as surgeons had a lull in patients coming through.

A few weeks later she and Bob went to Central Otago for a break and while in Cromwell Sue pulled from a knee that had been sore since the earthquake a 20 mm splinter. She plans to use it in an art work.

The aftermath has not been without its difficulties. Sue says she wants to talk to the police officer who rescued her but feels she will go to pieces if she does. The cast on her broken arm made her feel claustrophobic and had to be replaced with one that was smaller and lighter. 'It's totally irrational. Something else has taken over my mind and I have never felt like this before and I try to talk to it with my reason but it doesn't work. I need to work through that a little bit before I talk to these people. It still feels unreal. Like I'm watching an *Indiana Jones* movie.'

> 'A big part of my focus is the Cathedral. I think it's an important focal point for the community whether they are religious or not, and I would really like to see it rebuilt.'

Her experience in the earthquake has prompted a change in what she intends to do with her craft and art. 'I will still make quilts. I was doing very grand sorts of things that were in the public eye and I had a high profile. Since this has happened I know of five children, through people I know, who have lost parents. I want to make a quilt for specific kids. It's almost like returning to the roots of quilt making where you make a quilt to comfort and warm people. So I want to work locally and very low on the visibility scale and try to ease people's pain and that is probably by doing what I do best, which is to make quilts.'

Sue says a near-death experience certainly helps 'reprioritise'. 'It makes you realise what is really important. It's a way of refocusing on what you do and I want to try to help people. A lot of people are hurting a lot more than I am. I have [already] done a lot of exciting things. It's about everyday life. It's about relishing and savouring every single moment. I can be as happy here in Governors Bay as I can be anywhere in the world. I don't have to go to the other side of the world to have a wonderful time. I can have a wonderful time right where I am. I couldn't ask for anything more.'

Sue has also signed a pledge, circulated to show people are still committed to the city.

'I would really like to do something that would help rebuild the city. A big part of my focus is the Cathedral. I think it's an important focal point for the community whether they are religious or not, and I would really like to see it rebuilt. I feel this is my place now. I feel like I have roots that come out of my toes that go into the soil. I can't imagine living anywhere else in the world. You know the earth is doing what the earth does. That is how we got all those mountains out there. It's just the way it is. We have to be like the bees and lizards and live the best we can in the environment we are in.'

Not a great believer in the Judeo-Christian God, she feels that God exists in human beings. 'I saw these people rushing to help other people and not stopping to think of themselves. That whole sense of community and love and caring, to me, is what God is. A connection.'

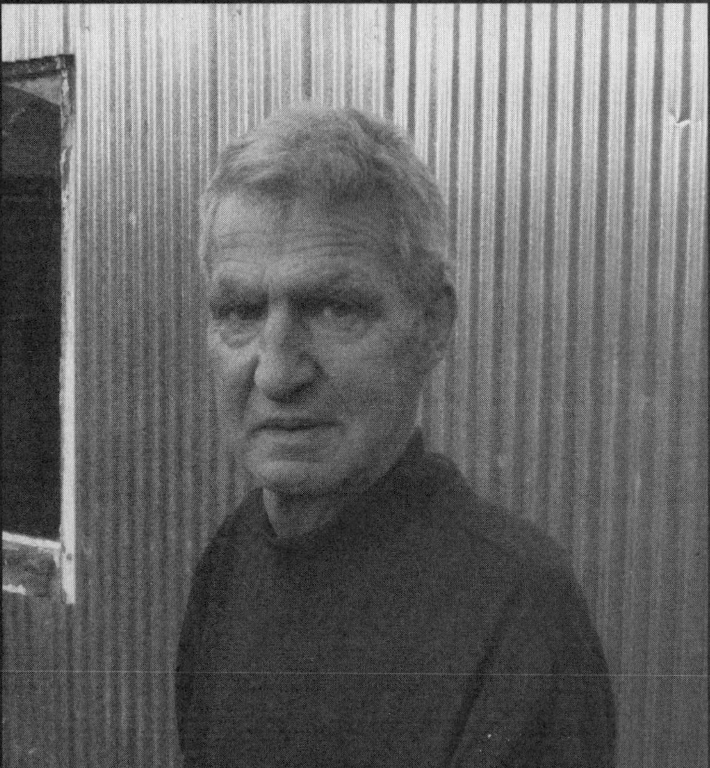

20

IAN REDDINGTON

'I was bloody lucky because it missed my skull by millimetres and I did not get the full impact on my back.'

IAN REDDINGTON IS tall, stooped and thin as a rake. Given his physique, it's ironic it should be food which him put in harm's way in the *Press* building on 22 February. His hurry to eat the mince pie he had bought from the popular Copenhagen Bakery in Armagh Street, one street away from the *Press*, made him overlook his normal precautions and had him sitting down at a cafeteria table on the third floor of the *Press* building at 12.51 p.m.

The former editor of the *Christchurch Star* had started back as a subeditor for *The Press* about a year before. He had been off work for three months with serious blood poisoning and had only been back at work for six weeks when the earthquake struck. Ian did not trust the *Press* building after it was damaged in the first Christchurch earthquake in September, 2010. He deliberately avoided the cafeteria because he did not like its single-entry-and-exit layout.

'I never went there for six months. In fact I would not walk along the side walls of the *Press*. I thought the *Press* building was dubious. I used to come down Worcester Street [onto which the *Press* building fronted] on the other side of the road and give the front a wide berth. Not because I was one of those people who had become neurotic over earthquake risks. Quite the contrary, but I did have some misgivings about the *Press* building. I thought I was taking a couple of reasonable commonsense steps by staying away from the bricks. I did have a thing about the third floor and walking close to the walls because of the bricks.'

On the day of the earthquake he had a hankering for a mince pie, which required a short walk to the Copenhagen Bakery, something of an institution for its speciality pies and delicious cakes. Ian, a mince pie connoisseur, says a good one is hard to find. 'For some reason I unthinkingly bowled up to the cafeteria to eat my pie and would have been out of there in five minutes, after having a quick read of the paper. For some reason I totally ignored whatever feeling I had about the building. I blame the bloody pie. You think of all the scenarios that could have happened that day and mine was dictated by a decision to buy a pie.'

Ian walked to a table close to the glass doors on the north side of the cafeteria and about as far away from the exit stairs as it was possible to get.

'I was sitting down and looked over my shoulder and felt the up and down and then saw the roof coming down. I had only managed two bites of the pie. The windows popped and within two seconds, I got hit by the roof. I was knocked to the ground, with the strut hitting my shoulder – you can see by the bruising where I was hit – and it went down and across my back fracturing the spine. I was bloody lucky because it missed my skull by millimetres and I did not get the full impact on my back.'

The strut had some more mischief in store, however. It trapped Ian's left hand on the table, which mostly held up under the pressure of the falling girder and floor above. His hand was caught up awkwardly behind him and he was left lying on the floor in a cavity about a metre high. His body had been dealt a severe thumping and his upper left arm was badly broken.

From his position he could see *Press* building supervisor Len McKenzie on his back among the debris and looking cramped. Len was reluctant to move for fear of bringing something down. The first helpers on the scene were staff from the Australian construction firm Ganellen, who had been putting the finishing touches to a new *Press* building on a plot near the cafeteria.

'The Ganellen guys got there reasonably quickly and it was a huge relief to know people were around. I thought it would be terrible to be trapped alone with nothing going on around me. An aftershock came just after the first one and then I sort of took stock and one of my reactions was sheer relief that I had survived.

'My first thoughts were that I could see Len and I had got out of it, but I didn't think anybody else could have got out of the cafeteria alive. Looking back on it, it looked like everything had come down and you couldn't conceive that anybody could have escaped that. Having seen how heavy that roof was, anybody under that would have got crushed. When I heard whispers about somebody having died I assumed it was Tim [Cronshaw (Chapter 7)], knowing where he was sitting.'

His hand was not initially particularly painful and neither was his shoulder but that was to change after about an hour when the numbness turned to red hot pain. 'The first part wasn't too bad. I don't know if the adrenalin helps in that situation or whether I just hadn't got to that point. I think numbness took over about half the time but the last hour and a half it was very painful every time I moved my shoulder. The bone leading up to the shoulder socket had snapped and broken away.'

An hour before, Ian had been subediting a film review about the movie *127 Hours*, a true story about lone American tramper Aron Ralston, who had his arm trapped by a falling rock and had to cut it off with his pocket knife. 'I was thinking some bastard might have to cut it off,' Ian says about his hand.

Ian got busy on trying to relieve the pressure on his hand by kicking away the legs from under the table. 'I got stuck in and tried to kick my way out of there. I had several goes at that but the weight was immovable. I abused the guys helping me. They sort of had a committee meeting at the start and there seemed to be long

'**The windows popped and within two seconds, I got hit by the roof. I was knocked to the ground, with the strut hitting my shoulder . . . it went down and across my back fracturing the spine.**'

periods when nothing was happening. I wasn't backward in saying, "What the hell is going on, you guys? You need to be pushing this along a bit and getting stuck in. You don't know if something is going to happen." I need to apologise to those brave souls. I can only say in my defence that my sense of urgency at that time was probably a little more elevated than theirs.'

He watched the roof in the second aftershock and was relieved to see that it did not appear to be falling any further. 'I did everything I could to kick the shit out of the underneath of the table but nothing moved at all. I made one huge effort to pull my hand out but it was fairly obvious that there was no room for anything to give. I worked out if someone could get a bar under the girder and push the table down it would just make enough room.

'I told Len and yelled it out to the rescuers as well. "Come on, get your arse in here." One guy, bless him, did, but he did not have enough room to lever the girder. It didn't work and I told him to get out because it wasn't safe.'

An added stress was that he could not ring his wife, the former *Sunday Star-Times* editor Cate Brett, who now works for the Law Commission, or any of his children, because his cellphone was still on his desk downstairs. Cate did not find out for three or four hours and the rest of his family did not know his whereabouts until he rang them from the hospital.

His rescuers decided the only way to release Ian's hand was to chip away the concrete above the girder. Ian says he could hear the work start above him and it seemed a long time before he could tell they were getting closer to where his hand was pinned.

'There came a point where I could tell they were getting close. I could tell by the sound and the amount of debris coming down. Then there was a breakthrough and a whole lot of stuff came down and the pressure relented on my hand and I used my other hand to slide it out. There was a big hurrah and I yelled out something grateful to the guys, I hope. The shoulder got very painful and the arm was basically useless. It was flopping around like a wet fish. I had no control over it because of the broken bone.

'I tried to get out myself out of the cavity but with one arm I couldn't. I kept tipping over and then they thrust in another plank and I moved onto the plank and they yanked me into the open air.'

The next part of the trip involved traversing the gap between the old *Press* building and the new, a gap with a four-storey drop. 'I looked down and saw. Oh my gosh. I was holding the plank with my right arm. They got me into the new building and then Mitch [Blunden] got me upright. They were all whooping and hollering and I gave them a little speech.'

Ian was delivered to the triage base in Latimer Square where he lay on his back under a big oak tree. 'We had this aftershock and the bloody tree was going all over the place. I thought, *I have just got out of the building and now this oak tree is going to fall on top of me.*'

His wedding ring was cut off his damaged hand, the fingers of which were swelling up. Ian says his hand was as flat as an egg flip when it emerged from under the girder. 'The hand is a miracle. It compressed down when I was up there and I thought if there is one serious repercussion out of this, I might lose the use of my hand.'

Ian was assessed by an orthopaedic surgeon and given morphine before being taken to hospital by ambulance, from where he could see the carnage and chaos. 'I thought as we were driving, *Oh my God, this is unbelievable. Thousands have died here today.* Stretches of the road felt like a war zone. The fire trucks, the helicopters gave the place that downtown Beirut feeling. I had a feeling this was a catastrophe of a big order. I thought a lot of people had died in the *Press* building.

'The hospital was pretty chaotic. Several times the building was swaying. They had these mobile X-ray units and then the power would go out. That was kind of like Beirut. I was dealt with and out of there in two hours. They put me in temporary plaster and told me to come back in three days. They didn't have enough room.

'It was a terrible night. I spent it with my daughter and her daughter in Hoon Hay. I didn't get an ounce of sleep because of the aftershocks. You felt the ground beneath us was in a continual state of flux. I was pretty spooked that night. It took quite a while to get over that feeling. I became one of those people who became overly anxious about where they are and was always strategising my exit. That was my little phobia for a while. Working out where I was going to put myself when the big one came.'

A week later he had surgery and was given a partial shoulder replacement. The muscles have yet to regain their strength and he still cannot lift up his arm. However tests show the shoulder is working well and he expects eventually to have a better shoulder than his previous one, which was plagued by arthritis. He has one fracture in his back and doctors are looking for another one.

'It's quite painful, my back. For the first six weeks after the earthquake I had trouble holding my torso up. Something has happened to the spine. My hand is fine. I still have some numbness but I got all the sensation back and not a thing is broken.'

In the months afterwards he had tried to make sense of his ordeal and why he was spared. 'I thought quite a bit about how small the difference is between surviving and not surviving in these sorts of incidents. And I wondered – I'm not saying I suddenly became religious or saw the hand of God in this – not the slightest, but it probably made me more fatalistic about things. When you are stuck in one of these situations you are in the lap of the gods. There is an incredibly small distance between life and death and I count myself lucky I was on the right side of this one.

'About three years ago I decided to pursue what Einstein was on about and what his theories were all about. You learn very quickly

> 'Is it fate, God's hand, the odds or just sheer luck that makes one person's outcome different from another's? I can do no better than say, I'm left with the view that what is, is.'

how benign things are on this planet in terms of the forces and energies that are happening in other places and in the make-up of the universe. Both these earthquakes have given me a glimpse of this and I kind of feel I have learned something. I remember the forces in the *Press* building that day and the upheaval that was going on almost in the blink of an eye. How powerful it was and thought this is what these people are talking about.'

Ian also wrote the following: 'It is sometimes tempting to try to find the words to describe the interaction of time and place amid the random chaos of events such as earthquakes. Is it fate, God's hand, the odds or just sheer luck that makes one person's outcome different from another's? I can do no better than say, I'm left with the view that what is, is.'

He finds it difficult to sleep because of discomfort from his injuries but he has no lingering traumatic feelings. 'I look back on it as kind of an interesting experience to reflect on occasionally. I don't go back very often to the earthquake. Essentially, I count my lucky stars. I'm still amazed not more people died in the *Press* building and the rest of the city.

'The truth is I got out of that building only because of the efforts and fortitude of the group from Ganellen joined by others from the *Press*. I'm told that about twenty minutes after they broke through the concrete, the roof under which I was trapped collapsed. Was that an example of the odds being on my side or was it, as I like to think, just what is, is. Whatever the answer, I don't think the remainder of that mince pie had such a happy ending.'

Kendyll with Jett (left) and Dita.

21

KENDYLL MITCHELL
JETT
DITA

'I was just in major shock. I rang my sister and apparently I just said, "I can't believe we are alive."'

KENDYLL MITCHELL, A young-looking, red-haired mother, was early for her appointment. She hated to be late for anything and today, 22 February, she was in the fifth-floor office of Relationship Services, 15 minutes before her appointment at 1 p.m. She and her two children, Jett, 4, and Dita, 10 months, waited quietly for the counsellors to finish their meeting in a room about 10 metres away. Jett was on one side of her and Dita was in her stroller.

It was their second meeting with counsellor Betty Inglewood in the CTV building in Madras Street. Kendyll had gone to Relationship Services to get help for Jett after he became anxious and sleepless following a severe aftershock which rattled their rented house in Spreydon. 'Jett was quite upset by the earthquake in September but seemed to be handling it. In mid-January we moved to a house in Spreydon and he lost the plot one night when we had a couple of [magnitude] three or fours. It sounded like a train had hit the house. It was just horrifically noisy. He wasn't coping. He would not sleep in his own bed. He was petrified of his bedroom. So we were all losing out on sleep. Relationship Services were doing free counselling, so we went there.'

Her partner Hayden Lamont, a machinery operator who is a sky-diver in his spare time, went to the first session and Kendyll remembers him saying the building should not be rocking just because a digger was working next door. Counsellor Betty had told Jett not to worry if the building shook. It was just because of the work going on next door.

'When it started I grabbed Jett because I knew he would be petrified. The longer it went the more I thought, *Shite*. You couldn't

223

move and I grabbed the front of the stroller. Then I saw an internal wall start to disintegrate. I thought we were all dead. Everyone started screaming.

'It felt like the building stayed in place and we got sucked down. It was a very fast falling feeling. And then I got knocked out on the fall. I don't remember hitting anything. Jett remembers everything and landed on his bum. I cut my leg and when I came around these two were covered in my blood. As soon as I opened my eyes, I thought I had to get out of there but my ankle was pinned by a piece of concrete.'

Jett told his mum afterwards that while she was knocked out, he had comforted Dita who was crying. When Kendyll regained consciousness, she found both of her children staring at her. Dita stopped crying. 'We were trapped in a sort of cubbyhole, a metre by a metre. All the contents of the building, pink batts, window frames, beams were around us. A steel beam went over our heads and it caused everything to "A-frame" around us. Dita had landed at my feet and her stroller, right up to her back, was embedded in the rubble. I removed the concrete and glass and got her out. I got into a crouch position because I couldn't stand up. It was too painful. I tried to remove the stuff over the top of us but it was just too heavy.'

She could see a patch of sky through the rubble and also the five-storey-tall stairwell, which was the only part of the building still standing. She began to worry that it might fall on them and that worry was replaced by another as she saw thick smoke rising from the rubble.

'I thought, *Oh my God, we have survived and now this.* You could hear muffled cries for help. The girl who was next to us in the waiting room was about two metres away and she was severely pinned. All she could do was move her hands. I was talking to her and asked her if she could use her cellphone. We were helpless.' [The girl was extracted from the rubble with back injuries but survived.]

Then she heard footsteps on the corrugated iron above them.

Two buses crushed in Colombo Street, looking north toward Cathedral Square. No casualties in the white bus but eight killed in the red bus. Ann Brower, the only survivor.

Iconic Bar (dark grey) building on the corner of Gloucester and Manchester Streets, where Amy Cooney was buried under rubble.

Sue Spigel waiting to be rescued from Christchurch Cathedral.
RICHARD COSGROVE, *THE PRESS*

Rescuers work quickly to free Marie Mackey from the rubble outside Bennetts Shoe Repair in Colombo Street. LOUISE AYLING

The rescue effort outside the former Ruben Blades salon. Glenn and Rochelle Prattley were trapped under the rubble. Glenn's partner Kelsey Moore and their baby Taneysha were killed by the collapsed veranda.

Sumner Road, near Evans Pass. Andre Chappell photographed the state of the road after he and fellow cyclists David Curtis and Symon Mitchell escaped the rock fall around them. ANDRE CHAPPELL

Their saviours were two workmen who had been on their lunch break from a job on a damaged church in Madras Street. 'They came and started pulling people out. So I yelled out to them and they pulled the rubble off us. I handed out Dita and Jett got quite upset because he thought he was not going to get out. I handed out Jett and he said, "Mum, you've got to get the stroller." Everyone got upset when they pulled the children out. The rumours of a crèche in the building may have stemmed from the sight of the children and some toys.'

'We were trapped in a sort of cubbyhole, a metre by a metre. All the contents of the building, pink batts, window frames, beams were around us. A steel beam went over our heads and it caused everything to "A-frame" around us.'

One of the workmen carried Kendyll off the building and then another helper, who turned out to be Mark Hoskins, one of Hayden's friends, took over and carried her for a short distance. Three women, two holding the children, went with her. Some other helpers took over carrying Kendyll, using a 'seat carry' lift, where she sat on the linked arms of the two people carrying her. 'That was awesome but they pulled my legs apart and I had two breaks at the front of my pelvis and the pain was unbearable. I was also telling them I did not want to go past any building.'

They arrived at the triage centre in Latimer Square with the children reasonably calm despite the sights of turmoil and the noise. Dita even went to sleep. Kendyll was assessed and waited in the square for an ambulance to take her to hospital. She began to go into shock, with her breathing starting to become rapid and shallow and her limbs feeling drained of energy, but just then Hayden arrived. He had raced across Christchurch on his bike after getting a phonecall from the friend who had helped carry Kendyll. Jett would not let him go once he had arrived.

In Christchurch Hospital Kendyll became number D211 and had

her pelvis X-rayed with a portable machine while the power came and went. She had a suspected break near her tailbone and doctors stitched up the gash in her leg by torchlight. Attempts to take her to an upstairs ward failed because of the power outages and she was taken to a waiting area for more X-rays. Through a slip-up caused by pressure on staff, Kendyll was mistakenly categorised as someone who could go home and return in the following days.

'It was bedlam and there were so many worse-off people.' She needed no persuading to go home with Hayden. 'We got home about 7 p.m. and I was just in major shock. I rang my sister and apparently I just said, "I can't believe we are alive." The kids were petrified with all the aftershocks. We decided to go to Timaru where we both have family. There was a major exodus.'

The next day she went to Timaru Hospital for some follow-up X-rays and found she had three breaks in her pelvis. She was admitted for six weeks' bed rest and was on crutches for ten weeks.

The stable ground of Timaru has been good for the family, she says. The aftershocks can be felt in Timaru but nothing like in Christchurch. 'Jett is doing amazingly well. He likes Timaru. He still has no idea of what he has been through but he hasn't needed any counselling.'

The knock to the head on 22 February has affected Kendyll's memory and she is seeing a specialist. She thinks she might have been knocked out for about 10 minutes and is worried about her short term memory, which she reckons is much worse than before the accident. But if she needs any reminding of her earthquake ordeal, she need only refer to her bulging file of photographs and magazine and newspaper stories.

'I really loved my kids but cherish them so much more now. We were so close to losing them. Hayden nearly lost all of us in one go.'

As she and the children were carried from the rubble, *Christchurch Star* photographer Geoff Sloan recorded much of the action. His photographs show helpers holding the children and two men carrying Kendyll, whose face is a picture of pain and shock. Kendyll remembers berating Sloan for photographing the moment but she is grateful now because she has an indelible record.

Kendyll, who has needed counselling for anxiety, says her injuries are healing and her attitude to life has changed considerably. 'I went through a phase of being quite angry because my life had to change. We had to move town, Hayden had to get a new job and we had to change pre-schools. I really loved my kids but cherish them so much more now. We were so close to losing them. Hayden nearly lost all of us in one go. Jett is constantly going, "Love you, Mum, love you, Mum." I'm now extremely close to Hayden. We are a very tightknit wee family.

'When the enormity of it hit, I did a week of "what ifs". What if I opened my eyes and the kids weren't there? What if we were by the car and something fell on us? What if we were in the lift? What if we were in the appointment? What if I didn't wake up? Then I got quite angry and then the post-traumatic stuff kicked in. But Jett has been a trouper right through.'

She remains anxious about buildings and doesn't like parking under shop verandas. She worries about ceilings and finds high-rise buildings a struggle. 'I was basically fearful of everything. I think, *If this happens, what will happen? Where do we go? Where will the children be safe?*'

Remaining is a feeling of enormous gratitude to all the people who helped her and the children from the wreckage of the building. 'A thank-you does not seem enough.'

Best friends Jackie Kinder (left) and Rachel Conley on their South Island tour.

22

JACKIE KINDER

'Knowing how close – literally feet away – I was from dying, I am not going to waste the second chance at life that I have been given.'

JACKIE KINDER AND Rachel Conley were on their last day in New Zealand when tragedy struck. Almost inseparable in friendship, they were only a metre or so apart when a heavy shop façade crumbled around them as they stood on a Christchurch street on 22 February. The metre was enough to mean that Jackie, a graphic designer, would survive and Rachel, a musical theatre major, would not.

The two met in a hostel in Wellington in March 2010 and quickly became best friends. Rachel, from Ohio, and Jackie, from Virginia, decided to make Wellington their New Zealand base and soon both had jobs. 'We somehow squeezed a lifetime worth of friendship into that single year we spent together in New Zealand. We were a good fit. Rachel was a very energetic, vibrant and optimistic person. She danced and sang a lot and was one of the most full-of-life people I have ever met,' says Jackie.

Rachel got work as a receptionist for a drama and dance school, and Jackie became nanny for a family of five. After a year, their working holiday visas ran out and they had nine days left to see the South Island. 'We managed to see the most stunning things we'd seen in our lifetimes. We toured Milford Sound in a three-storey boat, slept in our car outside a circus and skinny-dipped in a waist-deep stream by a highway.'

> 'Rachel was a very energetic, vibrant and optimistic person. She danced and sang a lot and was one of the most full-of-life people I have ever met.'

They arrived in Christchurch exhausted, with only two days to spare before their flight to Australia and Thailand where they planned to do some backpacking. They had been offered a house in Christchurch by friends in Wellington and arranged to see Christchurch on the last day of their stay in New Zealand.

They each wanted to get one more tattoo while travelling. Jackie decided to get hers in Christchurch but Rachel thought she would wait until Thailand. After walking around, they came across Southern Ink, on the corner of Colombo and St Asaph Streets, which Jackie describes as 'a clean and inviting little tattoo shop'. Jackie wanted the line 'Let it be', in Rachel's handwriting, tattooed on the back of her leg above the knee.

'That lyric was great for me because Rachel taught me to accept the things we can't change and move on knowing we're better for the decisions we've made, good or bad. Music was a big part of her life and Rachel was going to get the Beatles' line from "All You Need is Love", about always being in the place you're meant to be, tattooed on her. I now have both these tattoos. Her line is on my side below my heart.'

They made an appointment for later in the afternoon and then headed back onto the footpath.

'Rachel went out first and ambled down the footpath while I stayed back and made sure to close the heavy sliding door carefully. We were going to walk back to the hired car, return it to the airport, and hop on a bus back into town. Within seconds of shutting the door and following Rachel down the footpath, I felt a sudden, violent shaking sensation. I realised straight away what it was.

'My survival instinct kicked in immediately and I ran for the street. The noise is probably what I remember most, though I also remember that seeing straight and walking forward were impossible. There was a deafening roar and a shaking sensation that seemed to rattle me internally. After taking several unstable steps toward the street, I turned around to grab Rachel's hand and help her run with me, thinking she had followed my lead and was right behind me. She wasn't there.

'To my complete horror, she was frozen. She hadn't moved since the quake started, only seconds before. As I turned, hand outstretched to grab hers, I saw the concrete overhang and a cascade of brick and concrete pour down on her from the two-storey building above. It was fast but I knew immediately that she was gone.'

Jackie put her head into the open window of a car that had stopped in the middle of the road and clung to the vehicle. 'I braced myself for impact, thinking the building would surely topple my way and crush me like it had just done Rachel. That moment, though I thought it was my last, was far from scary. I felt a sense of peace and quiet, clarity and warmth surround me. I don't remember feeling any fear or any pain.'

Covered in thick dust and struggling to breathe, Jackie ran towards the heap of brick and concrete where her friend had been standing just moments before. She called out her name and a group of men arrived in response to her desperate shouts. They started frantically removing the debris from where Jackie pointed.

'I paced back and forth in the street, wanting to help yet feeling too stunned to act. I saw one of the men desperately reach into the pile, grab an exposed limb, feel her pulse, and then gently lay it back down – leaving her hand resting above the rubble. All the men quietly bowed their heads, dropped the bricks they still had in their hands, and slowly walked away.'

A man she knows only as Mike hugged her and told her nothing she could have done would have saved Rachel. He sat her down on the curb where she was joined by Matt and Sean Tonkin, two Christchurch brothers who had helped dig Rachel out. When Jackie was able to stand, Matt and Sean walked her back to her rental car and eventually took her to their parents' house in Parklands where she stayed the night.

'We pulled all the mattresses in the house into one room and we all slept there together so that I wouldn't have to be alone that first night. I didn't sleep at all, but being together with such genuine people made it bearable.'

The next day Jackie went to the police station to complete the official paperwork and that night flew to Wellington. 'While I was in Wellington, people baked me biscuits, brought me flowers, gave me a bed to sleep in and provided 24-hour emotional support. It was exactly where I needed to be to get my head around what had happened. Because Rachel was the only American killed, I was constantly in contact with the police, detectives, the US embassy and immigration officers.'

Jackie returned to Christchurch ten days later to help collect Rachel's DNA and fingerprint samples for identification purposes. Rachel's body was flown back to Ohio and cremated. Two weeks after the quake, the Te Whaea National Dance and Drama Centre, where Rachel had worked, held a memorial service which Jackie attended. 'The students played songs, had memorial dances for her and spoke beautiful words about her,' says Jackie.

Back in Staunton, Virginia, Jackie is living at home with her parents and is teaching (as a relief teacher) at a local school where her mother is the principal. She says her heart is still broken but she is thankful to be alive. 'Knowing how close – literally feet away – I was from dying, I am not going to waste the second chance at life that I have been given. Rachel will always be in my heart, as will the memory of those lovely New Zealand people who stood by me in such an unbelievable time of crisis. She loved everything about New Zealand, especially the people.

'Rachel was incredibly full of life and inspired many people. That was something I was trying to imitate while she was alive and now she's gone I've decided to live like she did, finding inspiration

> 'I see how devastated Rachel's parents still are and I'm very thankful to be alive for my parents' sake. She always told me, "Don't beat yourself up" whenever I felt bad about anything ridiculous. She even sewed a badge for me with those words.'

in every moment and every person. Making sure never to live with regret. Telling those you care about how much you love them. Going on daily adventures, big or small. Seeing beauty in everything and everyone.'

Although she felt guilty about surviving, the feeling did not last long, Jackie says. 'I see how devastated Rachel's parents still are and I'm very thankful to be alive for my parents' sake. She always told me, "Don't beat yourself up" whenever I felt bad about anything ridiculous. She even sewed a badge for me with those words.'

Jackie says she is recovering slowly and is seeing a counsellor for post-traumatic stress. She will soon be going to Scotland and England to visit Rachel's friends there. She also wants to come back to Wellington to live.

'Like I said, I intend to continue my thirst for travel and new adventures.'

Top, from left: Cyclists Symon Mitchell, Andre Chappell and David Curtis.
Above: Cable operator for the Christchurch Gondola, Nick Carson.

23

DAVID CURTIS
NICK CARSON

'The big ones had such a big mass they were doing a slow cartwheel. Others were rushing through and, to my horror, hurtling towards me.'

THE PORT HILLS overlooking Christchurch are one of the city's great assets. Formed as the result of a huge volcanic eruption eons ago, the cliffs and ridges make a wonderful playground for the active.

For lean, tanned former police officer and super-fit cyclist David Curtis, the hills were a superb training route. On 22 February, he and mates and fellow cyclists Andre Chappell, also a former policeman, and Symon Mitchell, a fireman, left home about 11 a.m. to bike what Christchurch cyclists call the 'short bays' route. It takes cyclists high up along the edge of Lyttelton harbour, which is the flooded caldera of the ancient volcano. It was a perfect day for cycling and as they headed up the road, steadily increasing the pace, they watched a gleaming white passenger liner glide gracefully out of the harbour. The ride was going to take about two hours, including a stop for a coffee.

They were about 800 metres from the top of Evans Pass, from where they would have a downhill ride to the seaside suburb of Sumner, when the earthquake struck. Above them was a steep tussock-clad slope and higher up a semi-circle of cliffs and bluffs.

'I was out in front by about fifty metres, with Andre about fifty metres back and Symon about two hundred metres behind Andre,' says David, who was a top Wellington triathlete in his youth. He, like Andre, is one of the top four or five cyclists in their age group in Canterbury.

'When the quake first hit I thought it was a strong breeze. It made me stop on the bike and then it was like a sonic boom. A massive blast of hot air seemed to come off the cliffs above. It blasted me about three metres from the left hand to the right hand curve of the road. I ended up on the verge on the other side of the road still standing on my bike. I turned and looked up the hill and the big rocks right around the summit were smoking. Dust and what seemed to be smoke was rising. Hundreds of boulders came down. Some the size of buses, some as big as cars and then smaller ones. Some dropped and bounced 30 metres each time they hit the ground. The big ones had such a big mass they were doing a slow cartwheel. Others were rushing through and, to my horror, hurtling towards me.'

By this time Andre had caught up with him and yelled out to David that he should run for it.

'He jumped over the fence and hid in the tussock and I thought that was a crazy place to be because you couldn't see anything coming. So I just stood on the road and watched them come down. I didn't have to move. They came down beside me, to the right of me, in front of me. The very big boulders when they hit the road carried on and down the hill.

'Some went into the gulley where Andre was and my immediate thought was he had been crushed to death. I went across and called out and he popped his head out of the tussock and I was delighted he was OK. Symon came around the corner and we all stood there and thought, *Wow.*'

Andre had a camera and took some photos of the huge dents in the road. The cyclists then discussed whether they should carry on to the pass, only a tantalising 800 metres away. David was of the view it was too dangerous because of the sheer cliffs rising directly above the road and argued they should head back to Lyttelton township, the way they had come. The other two wanted to continue, and carried the day.

'We stood there for three or four minutes and I said, "All right, we will go ahead," but I wasn't comfortable. By this time the road was covered in boulders from the first quake and we carried our bikes up and had only just gone around the corner when the first aftershock hit. Boulders so big they did not lose contact with the ground came through.'

Symon yelled out that they should hug the cliff and taking their bikes they sought the precarious shelter of a cliff face which could itself have crumbled at any moment. 'I immediately had a sense that I was doomed. It was interesting because there was no panic. The scale of where we were was amazing. There was a sense of being trapped because we had nowhere to go because we had the drop off on the right and then the cliff face. The road was already strewn with boulders, and rocks were coming down and luckily they were smashing down on the road around us.

'We had nowhere to go because we had the drop off on the right and then the cliff face. The road was already strewn with boulders, and rocks were coming down and luckily they were smashing down on the road around us.'

'You couldn't see the rocks coming and the rocks were appearing and smashing down. They could have dropped straight down on us. We stood there for about two or three minutes, worried the whole cliff face was moving, and with just a sensation that we were doomed. We were quiet. It was just so big that there was no room for panic. There was nothing you could do except just wait. It's really amazing we survived.

'I said, "Let's run," and we were hopping along in our cycling shoes, skipping along. We had our bikes on our shoulders and we came around this corner and there was a petrol tanker, abandoned with its engine still running and surrounded by rocks. What was the chance of seeing a petrol tanker there? We went past it and we thought *If a boulder comes down now you've got a petrol tanker to deal with.* We got past that and then found ourselves in a clear space. We met a police officer at the top and he was amazed to see us.'

But they were not in the clear just yet. When they reached Sumner they saw a queue of cars that looked to be heading up the pass towards Lyttelton and told drivers not to go any further. As they were warning the drivers, a man rushed up to say the sea was rushing out of Sumner and a tsunami was on the way.

'We ran up a side street and there were women standing with little kids at the gates. We said there might be a tsunami coming. They were all terrified. There would have been 50 people there and mothers carrying kids and these women were saying, "My name is Donna and this is Timmy if anything happens." So we all stood on higher ground telling each other what our names were.'

But fortunately the tsunami never eventuated and they began the cycle home through a devastated city. David saw a van on Clifton Hill crushed by a rock and further around the winding route into the city he saw a helicopter had landed at Redcliffs School and all the children lined up on the school ground. Behind the school a huge section of the cliffs that gave the suburb its name had crashed down, smashing trees and leaving some nearby houses battered and broken.

'The estuary had no water and was all liquefacted. The bridge had dropped and Ferry Road was under a metre of water. Thousands of people were walking out of town and we biked on through. Everyone was orderly. No panic.'

David says he was quite emotional when he arrived at his house in Fendalton. 'I really felt as though I had dodged a bullet.'

He then had an anxious couple of hours waiting before he heard from his daughter who was in the IRD building, opposite the collapsed CTV building in Madras Street when the earthquake hit. Symon had to go straight to work, helping to co-ordinate the rescue.

While David Curtis and his mates were sheltering against the cliff face, on the other side of the hill range Nick Carson was also taking evasive action.

Carson, a cable operator for the Christchurch Gondola – which takes sightseers from a base station in the Heathcote Valley to a large facility near Mt Cavendish for spectacular views of Christchurch and Banks Peninsula – was working behind the base station when the earthquake hit. He had been first to arrive at work that morning and had put 18 cabins on the gondola cable before completing safety checks. The gondola opened to the public at 10 a.m. but because the top station was in cloud he didn't expect a lot of custom.

'I decided to get the weed-eater out and went out the back where there is a big lawn. I'd been doing it for about twenty minutes and because I was wearing earmuffs and also because of the noise from the weed-eater I did not hear the sound when it hit. People said it was a huge boom but I didn't hear it. It felt like I just got lifted and then I looked around and next thing I saw was big boulders coming off Castle Rock [a rocky peak to the west].'

The gondola cable supports are spaced out along a valley which is a natural conduit for falling rocks. Having a master's in Geology did not change Nick's perception of what was happening. 'It's all bedrock so there are just going to be big boulders,' he says.

Nor did he think about his brother Benjamin, a Royal New Zealand Air Force helicopter crewman who was killed in April 2010, when his Iroquois crashed near Wellington on its way to a flypast for Anzac Day commemorations. 'I thought about him afterwards but not while it was all happening.'

Rocks, some the size of cars, were coming off Castle Rock in a potentially lethal cascade. 'I thought I'd better make sure everyone is out of the foyer area [of the base station] because people sheltering inside could get taken out. I ran down the slope and through the loading bay door and as I came through one of those glass panels fell down. They are six-foot-square panels and would have killed anybody underneath them.

'I couldn't see anyone in the foyer so headed out along the way the gondola cabins come in. There is a fence round the back to prevent the kids getting hit by cabins because they come in so low to the ground. As I came through the back way a huge boulder came through and wiped out the gate two metres away from the building. I was amazed that the fence stopped it.

'I jumped up on the fence and another boulder came through and demolished some cabbage trees. There were big thumps when they hit. I was standing on top of the fence and I thought, *I'm not going to move from here unless I see something coming straight for me.* There wasn't much high ground to go to. I looked out for more boulders but couldn't see any more coming. The boulders seemed to have come from the road. They bounced everywhere and got quite a lot of air.'

The aftershocks brought down more boulders but very few large ones got as far as the gondola station. Nick watched a big one come down from Castle Rock and smash through a pine tree.

After the risk from boulders had reduced, Nick's next thought was for the gondola passengers, as the cable can't operate without power. The operation has an emergency generator but staff are not allowed to use it in an earthquake. Fortunately, only one gondola cabin was stuck on the cable, about 100 metres from the base station and about 20 metres from the ground.

'I had seen the two people and they were doing what we call "the washing machine" – the cabin just swings around in a circle. I radioed the top station and asked them how many they had sent down. They said they hadn't had anyone for ages. So I established reasonably quickly that they were the only ones. I walked up carefully to be underneath the cabin.'

He had to yell at the cabin's occupants to get them to open their window and he explained about the earthquake. They were an American couple in their sixties and looked a bit puzzled. 'I offered them water and clothing and they said they were fine. I was a bit surprised they were not freaked out.'

Nick was then winched up to the top of the cabin and lowered into position for the rescue. 'You sort of swing into the cabin. The couple seemed quite happy and I got their harnesses and asked them who would like to go first. The wife said, "Apparently I have to because he wants to take photos."'

Before Nick and other staff went to check on the top station, he went home to check on his mother. Her house was a bombsite, with part of the house twisted off its lower storey and the inside covered in glass. It would eventually be red-stickered. His mother wasn't there but Nick learned his uncle had already picked her up and taken her to his house. Nick then carried on to the gondola's top station, which he also found in a bad way when he reached it. 'The top floor was 200 mm deep in water as the sprinkler pipes had broken. You could hear water dripping through the whole place.'

Nick says it was lucky the day was cloudy as the whole line could have been full of occupied gondolas had the weather been sunny. The experience was not one of those life-changing moments, he adds. 'We trained for it and I didn't think it was anything special.'

David, who until recently owned a Harcourts real estate franchise, still gets emotional when he talks about his near-death experience and that surprises him as he has not previously been that way inclined. He was in the Police dive squad and also in the Blue Squad during the Springbok tour. As a detective he has been in what he calls 'a lot of extreme situations'. When he went to Blenheim after the earthquake he met a friend who gave him a hug.

'I broke down. I was surprised by the emotion of it. I couldn't understand it. I felt embarrassed by it. But it's your own mortality, isn't it. We all really felt we had a second chance at life and I think part of the emotion is from that feeling. Appreciating things a bit more.'

INDEX

ACC 139
Adam and Eve Adult Supplies (shop), Christchurch 77
Adams, The Revd Fr John 61
Air New Zealand 28-9
Aoraki-Mt Cook 111
Armagh Street, Christchurch 69, 109, 167-8, 170, 213
Arts Centre, Christchurch 186
Askew, James 160
Auckland 70, 72, 120, 131, 188
Auckland Hospital 188
Auckland orthopaedic team 132
Aurora Centre, Burnside High School 41
Australia 35, 58, 152, 231
Avon River 99, 181
Avondale, Christchurch 177
Avonhead, Christchurch 171

Banks Peninsula 37, 60, 242
Bealey Avenue, Christchurch 110
Beck, The Very Revd Peter 206
Beijing, China 159
Belcher, Jayne 171
Bennetts Shoe Repairs, Christchurch 139-40
Berkeley University, California 46
Blenheim 245
Blue Squad (Police) 245
Blunden, Mitch 217
Bodkin, Ann 96-105, 154
Bodkin, Bill and Shirley 100
Bodkin, Ross 101
Bouda, Simon 103
Boxing Day 2010 aftershocks, Canterbury 94, 117, 177
Brett, Cate 216
Brisbane, Australia 41
Brower, Ann 42-50
Burgess, Annette 57-8, 60
Burnham Army Camp 70
Burnside High School 41, 70
Burwood Hospital Spinal Unit 48-9, 83, 121-3, 133, 139, 142, 180

Cambridge Terrace, Christchurch 55, 149, 167, 187

Cameron, Grant 46, 84, 111-13
Canada 22
Canterbury 11, 14, 46, 132, 159, 239
Canterbury Earthquake Recovery Authority 132
Canterbury Fire Service 171
Canterbury Plains 11
Canterbury Television (CTV) 21, 129
Carson, Nick 236-45
Cashel Street, Christchurch 94, 160-1
Cashmere Hill 206
Castle Rock 241-2
Cathedral Square, Christchurch 177
CBS News (New York) 62
Central Otago 207
Central Park, New York 62
Channel 9 TV (Australia) 103
Chappell, Andre 236, 239-40
Chicago, USA 194
China 159, 162
Chinmoy, Sri 77
Chivell, Dave 119
Christchurch 11-13, 16, 21-3, 29-31, 41, 67, 131-2, 134, 159, 162, 185-6, 188-9, 193-4, 203-4, 231-2
Christchurch Boys' High School 117
Christchurch Casino 56
Christchurch Cathedral 91, 161, 203-9
Christchurch Central Fire Station 58
Christchurch earthquakes 2010 and 2011 12, 55, 129, 159, 213
Christchurch Gondola 236, 242-5
Christchurch Hospital 27-8, 30, 48-9, 101, 104, 119, 141-2, 152, 154, 180, 187
Christchurch Polytechnic 36
Christchurch Press see Press
Christchurch Star 129, 213, 226
Chua Hospital 29
Church of Christ the King (Catholic) 55
City Art Gallery, Christchurch 101

Civil Defence Headquarters 101, 134
Clyde Road, Fendalton, Christchurch 117, 124
Coker, Brian 154
Collins and Harman 94
Colombo Street, Christchurch 49, 69, 77-9, 81, 83, 109, 112, 140, 144, 155, 167
Conley, Rachel 80, 81, 228-35
Cooney, Amy 33-41
Cooper, Emily 13
Copenhagen Bakery 213
Copthorne Hotel 110
Countdown Supermarket, Moorhouse Avenue 194
Cromwell 207
Cronshaw, Tim 87-93, 178-9, 214
CTV (Canterbury Television) 21, 129
CTV building 13, 21-31, 50, 67-72, 129-35, 159-63, 185-9, 223-7, 242
Cullen, Gordon 164-5, 167-72
Cultural Revolution (China) 159
Curran, Bryce 154
Curtis, David 236-43

Dalai Lama 49-50
Dallington, Christchurch 152
Darfield 11
Dunedin 83, 105, 194
Dunedin Hospital 196
Duns Ltd 167
Durham Street, Christchurch 206
Dutch Reformed Church 162

Earthquake Commission 117, 139
Economist 46
Edgeware, Christchurch 193
Education Review Office 99
Edwards, Beverley 123
English language students 21
English language teachers 67
English studies 22, 27, 29, 67, 185, 189
Environment Canterbury 110
Essex, UK 149
Europe 103, 143

246 TRAPPED

Evans, Kate 139, 141, 144
Evans, Petter 139, 141–2, 144–5
Evans Pass 239

Faithfull, Isobel 153
Faithfull, Jacqui 149, 151–5
Faithfull, Jim 146–55
Faithfull, Ollie 153
February 22, 2011 earthquake 35, 45, 117, 139, 193
Fendalton, Christchurch 117, 242
Ferry Road, Christchurch 242
Flintoff, Kim 57–9
Forsyth Barr Building 69, 109, 113, 167, 169, 171, 172
Fortune, Lenny 160
Fyfe, Tom 111

Ganellen Construction Co. 91–2, 94, 214, 219
GCA Lawyers 110–11
Gestalt Institute 167
Gilbert, Jaime Robert McDowell 35–41
Gilbert, Levi 35
Gilbert, Robert 41
Gloucester Street, Christchurch 35, 92
Godkin, Ron 68–9
Godoy, Pablo 130
Goodall, Dwayne 57
Governors Bay 207–8
Great Hall (Arts Centre) 186
Green, Rob 46–8
Greenslade, Chris 52, 55–62
Greenslade, Emma (née Howard) 52–62, 187
Grice, Ben 117, 120–1
Grice, Charlotte 117
Grice, Helen 115–24, 144
Grice, Henry 117–19
Grice, Matthew 117
Grice, Simon 117
Grottis, Barry 129, 131
Guiney, Helen 151–2, 154

Hagley Park 13, 101, 141
Haley, Betsy 207
Hamlet 36, 41
Hanmer Springs 22
Hanrahan, Sister Mary 121
Harcourts Real Estate 245
Hawaii 181
Haynes, John 110–13
Heathcote Valley 89, 242
Heffernan, Chris 57
Herbert, Nick 180

Hereford Street, Christchurch 38
High Country Outdoors Recreation shop 140
Hill, Clifton 242
Hirauchi, Yoshiko 70, 185–9
Holden, Andrew 16
Holmes, Nicola 167
Hoon Hay 218
Hornby, Christchurch 84
Hornby Mall 40
Horsley, David 21, 64–72, 186
Horsley, Michael 68
Hoskins, Mark 225
Howard, Emma *see* Greenslade, Emma (née Howard)

Iconic Bar 35–6
India 35
Inglewood, Betty 223
IRD building 71, 242
Iroquois helicopters 241
Iwakura, Rika 18–31

Japan 16, 22, 25, 29–30, 62, 71–2, 170, 188, 207
Japanese Consul 69
Japanese Consular Office 169
Japanese Embassy 29, 71
Japanese media 28, 71
Japanese speakers 70
Japanese students 22

Kawahata, Kuniaki 22
Kawahata, Kyoko 22
Kawai, Shoichi 69, 170
Kilmore Street, Christchurch 161
Kinder, Jackie 80–1, 228–35
King, Bruce 91
King's Education Language School 21–3, 68–9, 185–6
Kiyu, Tomoko 21, 24
Knox Church 110
Koshi Rehabilitation Hospital, Toyama 30

Lamont, Hayden 223, 225–7
Latimer Square 69, 72, 131–2, 141, 160, 217, 225
Lead Rubber Bearings (technology) 134
Levin, Brenda 167, 170–1
Li-Stacey, Diana 169, 171–2
Lichfield Street 46, 141, 194
Lincoln, Canterbury 56, 60
Lincoln University 46

Lindsay, Adrienne 13, 91, 179–80
Little River, Banks Peninsula 37–9
Littlewood, Chris 106–13
Lotus Heart Restaurant 77, 79, 81
Lyttelton 239–41

Mackey, Marie 123, 136–45
Macpac shop 140
Madras Street, Christchurch 160
Malaysia 67
Malcolm, Anne 126–35
Malcolm, Jen 131–2
Malcolm, Jo 132
Malcolm, Robyn 132
Manchester Street, Christchurch 35–6, 38, 141, 194
Marsden, Gabriel 169
Martin, Paul 207
Masutani, Norika 26, 28, 70
Matsuta, Yuki 188
McDonald, Philip 57–8, 62
McEachen, Matti 78–83
McKenzie, Len 179, 214–16
Methven, Canterbury 188
Michigan, USA 203
Minami, Yukio 18–31
Ministry of Education 99
Mitchell, Dita 220–27
Mitchell, Jett 220–7
Mitchell, Kendyll 220–7
Mitchell, Symon 236, 239–42
Moore, Kelsey 193–8
Moorhouse Avenue, Christchurch 196
Morse code 103
Mosgiel, Otago 193, 196
Mt Cavendish 242
Mt Fuji 185

National Academy of Singing and Dramatic Art 36
New South Wales, Australia 101, 103
New Zealand 27, 46, 50, 67, 70, 111, 159, 186, 189, 203, 231–2, 234
New Zealand Institute of Sport 129
New Zealand Law Commission 216
North Parkes Mine accident, NSW 101

INDEX   247

O'Brien, Natalie 35
Ohio, USA 231, 234
Okuda, Hamako 30
Okuda, Kento 18–31
Otago Polytechnic 194
Outrageous Fortune 132

Pak'nSave Supermarket 78
Parker, Bob (Mayor) 11–12, 121
Parker, Ros 57
Parkin, Matt 74–84
Parkin, Seth 83
Parklands, Christchurch 186, 233
PGC building *see* Pyne Gould Corporation building
Piper, George 91, 179
Port Hills 45, 239
Porter, Rose 186
Post, Ed 164–72
Prattley, Glenn 190–8
Prattley, Rochelle 190–8
Prattley, Taneysha 193–8
Press building 13, 89–94, 177–80, 213–19
Press (newspaper) 13, 16, 89, 91–4, 111, 177, 213, 219
Putra, Dr Lydia Johns (Australian urological surgeon) 154
Pyne Gould Corporation building 50, 55–63, 99–105, 112, 149–55, 167–9, 172, 187

Queen's High School, Dunedin 194
Queenstown 31

Rae, Ian 168–9, 171
Ralston, Aron 214
Rarotonga 62
Red Cross 196
Redcliffs School 242
Redcliffs Supermarket 45
Reddington, Ian 179, 210–19
Redwood, Christchurch 161
Reeves, Stacey 180
Reid, Lyn 89–90, 92–3, 175, 177–81
Reid, Murray 181
Relationship Services Counselling Agency 129, 133, 159, 223
Riccarton, Christchurch 62, 83
Richardson, Graham 96, 99, 101–5

Robinson, Dr Bill 134
Robinson Seismic Ltd 134
Rodwell, Paul 16, 26–7
Rolleston, Canterbury 101
Royal Commission of Inquiry 50, 63, 172
Royal New Zealand Air Force 241
Ruben Blades salon 195
Rule, Steve 41, 58–60

Sato, Hiroko 70, 183, 185–9
Scobie, Liz 119
Scobie, Rupert 117–19
Scott, Chris 187–8
Scott, Rebecca 188
Sendai earthquake, 2011 (Japan) 72
Sendai tsunami, 2011 (Japan) 62
September 4, 2011 Canterbury earthquake 56, 68, 77, 83, 94, 110–11, 117, 133–4, 149, 167, 177–8, 193–4
Service, Emma 74–84
Sherwood Estate 139
Siave, Sam 37–8
Singapore 119
Singapore Airlines 16
Singh, Bonnie 74–84
Sloan, Geoff 226
Sopoaga, Ashei 37–8
South Island 120, 228, 231
Southern Cross Hotel 105
Southern Ink tattoo studio 77–84, 232
Southland 99–100
Spigel, Betsy 207
Spigel, Bob 203, 206–7
Spigel, Sue 200–9
Spreydon 223
St Asaph Street, Christchurch 77, 232
Starship Hospital, Auckland 196
Staunton, Virginia 234
Stewart, Cam 140–1
Stewart, Cory 60
Stick, Beverley 155
Stick, Earl 155
students, English language 21
Summit Road, Christchurch 186
Sumner, Christchurch 45, 239, 241–2
Sutton, Jo 132
Sutton, Roger 132
Sydenham, Christchurch 120
Sydney, Australia 162

Tairakena, Te Taki (Wally) 21–2
Tang, Qing 156–63
Tankersley, Louise 130–1, 159–60
Tauranga 67–8
Taylor, Brian 22
teachers, English language 67
TFCL *see* Toyama College of Foreign Languages
Tonkin, Matt 233
Tonkin, Sean 233
Toyama, Japan 16, 21–3, 25, 27–9, 67, 70, 188
Toyama College of Foreign Languages 16, 21–2, 31, 67, 185
Tuam Street, Christchurch 46
TV3 196
Twin Towers (New York) 111, 178 *see also* World Trade Center

Uchihira, Yurika 23, 25, 27, 31
United States 30, 48, 103
University of Canterbury 45, 67, 132, 134, 159
unreinforced masonry (URM) buildings 50, 193
Urakami, Susan 16
US Embassy officers 234

Victoria Park 18
Victoria Square 170
Villa Maria College 121
Virginia, USA 231, 234
Vos, Ann 151–2

Waipara 139, 141
Wairarapa Stream 118
Wairewa marae 39
Walker, Maurice 112
Wall, Nick 57–8
Wellington 109, 132, 134, 231–5, 241
Wellington Hospital 28
West Melton, Canterbury 171
White, Glen 57
Woolston, Christchurch 35
Worcester Street, Christchurch 194, 213
World Cup, Rugby, 2011 36
World Trade Center (New York) 111, 203
Wuyuan, Tang 159

X-rays 83, 120, 196, 226

Yangtang, China 159